Contradicting Biblical Conjecture about the Crucifiction

By Gregory Heary

Some Christians tell me that I must absolutely believe that Jesus was crucified, died for my sins and was resurrected, or else. Or else I will go to hell forever. Yet none of the prophets before Jesus ever believed in or taught this doctrine, including Jesus! In the bible and outside of the bible Jesus never said people have to believe he is God, or the son of God, or was crucified, died or was risen in order to attain salvation. Saul/Paul is the one who is first documented to have started preaching this. If I were a judge deciding whether a person was guilty of murder or not I would need evidence and witnesses before believing the accusations, or else I would be considered unjust for believing the hear-say; which is actually the root word heresy comes from. Especially if the Jewish people as a whole are being blamed for this murder, I would definitely need solid irrefutable proof lest I blame innocents. Of course Jews have done many bad things, but they aren't guilty for all they are charged with. If the alleged crucifixion, death and resurrection really happened and I have to believe how the bible says it happened in order to go to heaven, then how does the bible say it happened? I'm told the authors of the gospels in the bible were witnesses to the alleged crucifixion, death and resurrection; but the gospel of Mark says there were no witnesses. Whether you believe in the bible or not we have to be fair and let the bible tell its side(s) of the story. Too often we get told a non-biblical Easter story narrative instead of the biblical version(s) of events. Therefore let us examine the biblical text horizontally with critical analysis putting the gospels side by side and God-willing we will know the plain and simple truth when we read it. Despite what I was told and used to believe about Jesus the bible paints a different picture than the Easter story they share in churches and mass media. After genuine study it is clear to the sincere reader that the biblical version of the crucifixtion contradicts the famous Easter story and each biblical gospel contradicts the other biblical gospels information about the alleged crime. This book proves that the crucifiction story which Christians are told and believe is biblical fact has no basis from the bible and is mythological conjecture composed of bits and pieces of some gospel texts wherein most biblical text on the subject is ignored because the 4 New Testament gospels contradict each other when describing the same alleged event. Basically to believe the Easter story requires one to disbelieve in most of the biblical text concerning the plot against Jesus. I guarantee that if you believe Jesus was crucified, died and rose again then you don't believe what the bible says regarding that. Yet sadly the Easter story propagators fool people into thinking their story is biblically based. If the crucifiction story is true then I'd be a fool to disbelieve in it and if believing in it is the way to heaven then I'd be damned for doubting or disbelieving. Thus I offer my analysis in the hopes that a dialogue will begin and we all can be guided to the truth of what happened to Jesus the prophet of God.

Let us start our study with what the bible says about the alleged crucifixion beginning with what Jesus had prophesied before the events are said to have taken place. As a Christian missionary repeatedly told me, "*you will know the truth when you read it*" so with that advice let us read the bible to see if we can recognize it to be the truth as the Christian told me I would. Remember we cannot let emotions or preconceived notions influence our judgment. Whether you currently believe the bible to be true or false I ask that you read the verses with an open mind free of pre-dispositions and let the bible speak for itself and tell us its own version of what really happened to Jesus. The English New International Version of the bible Matthew 12:38-40 says:

> "*38 Then some of the Pharisees and teachers of the law said to him, "Teacher, we want to see a sign from you. 39 He answered, "A wicked and adulterous generation asks for a sign! But none will be given it except the sign of the prophet Jonah. 40 For as Jonah was three days and three nights in the belly of a huge fish, so the Son of Man will be three days and three nights in the heart of the earth.*"

The gospel of Matthew has Jesus say "Son of Man" here, since Jesus had no human father perhaps it is a reference to the first man we are all descended from, called Adam. This phrase would imply that Jesus is human and was not created before Adam. The sign or miracle Jesus promises to the Pharisees will be the sign of Jonah. Jonah was a prophet who disobeyed God and went in a boat traveling away from the place God told him to preach at. When on the boat a storm arose and Jonah knew it was because God was displeased with him so he volunteered to be thrown overboard. The sailors didn't think Jonah was the reason for the storm but after casting lots finally agreed to throw him overboard. Keep in mind he volunteered, when a person voluntarily sacrifices themselves they don't have to be beat, whipped or coerced. In fact according to the bible and Jewish sacrifices, if any bones on the creature being sacrificed are broken before their death then it makes that sacrifice unacceptable and invalid. Jonah was alive and thrown overboard, instead of drowning miraculously he was swallowed by a whale without dying. Miraculously he wasn't digested and the bible says after 3 days and 3 nights Jonah was spit out of the whale onto earth having been alive the entire time. Truly an amazing miracle. The miracle was not the amount of time that passed, but the fact that Jonah remained alive. Surviving was the sign. Typically if you get thrown overboard you die, or if you're eaten by a whale you die, or if you spend time in the belly of a whale you die, or if you get spit out by a whale you die, but Jonah stayed alive the entire time by the will of God. God saved Jonah, if Jesus were God then when talking about Jonah he would have said that he saved Jonah. But Jesus didn't save Jonah because he is not God. If Jesus said the Pharisees would get the sign/miracle of Jonah then it meant Jesus would miraculously be alive unnaturally even when there would be many reasons to think he had died. In response many Christians might say, "no it was the 3 days and 3 nights that matches the 3 day theory of Jesus rising on Sun-day". Ok let's count, if you believe Jesus died Friday that's Friday night, Saturday day, Saturday night and Sunday morning he is said to be risen. That's not 3 days and 3 nights, it's only 2 nights and 1 day. If you are one who doesn't believe in "Good Friday" and think all the churches got it wrong believing those who say Thursday are right. Let's count, Thursday night, Friday day, Friday night, Saturday day, Saturday night and risen on Sun-day. That's 3 nights and 2 days, also if Jesus was crucified on Thursday then the Sabbath would have been over 24 hours away, so Jesus wouldn't have been taken down for over 24 hours. In response some will say it was a special holiday Sabbath. However special holiday Sabbaths only took place during the 7th month of the Jewish calendar whereas Passover took place during the 1st month. Even if that were the case, which it can't be, it would mean that Jesus had celebrated the Passover a day early. Either way it doesn't add up and I don't believe the prophet Jesus was a liar. Also keep in mind that the "Son of Man" is said to be "in the heart of the earth" while even according to Christians Jesus was never "in the heart of the earth" but Christians say he was in a sepulcher above the ground. Perhaps this sign was a reference to a miracle Jesus did to someone else raising them from the dead instead of the alleged crucifixion of Jesus. Or maybe that bible verse in Matthew just isn't true. On the other hand the gospel of Mark also contains a similar reading of this encounter between Jesus and the Pharisees with a major difference. Mark 8:11-13 say:

> *11 The Pharisees came and began to question Jesus. To test him, they asked him for a sign from heaven. 12 He sighed deeply and said, "Why does this generation ask for a sign? Truly I tell you, no sign will be given to it." 13 Then he left them, got back into the boat and crossed to the other side."*

Now this is a blatant biblical contradiction. Mark says Jesus tells the Pharisees there will be no sign given, while Matthew says Jesus promised a sign to the Pharisees. Either Jesus did or he didn't, so either Matthew or Mark is lying about Jesus, at the very least one of these biblical verses is wrong. They both portray the same event yet have completely different versions of Jesus. They cannot be different events because the later event would have the Pharisees expose Jesus for changing his position which they would have used to declare him a hypocrite. Certainly Jesus didn't lie or flip-flop. Neither do people inspired by God contradict each other. This is why it is important to read the bible horizontally sometimes instead of vertically. Vertically reading the bible is when a person reads an entire gospel one after another. Horizontally reading is when one reads the bible chronologically reading the gospels side by side hearing what all the gospels say about the same event before reading about the next event. When reading the gospels side by side they show themselves to be contradictory and at odds with each other. When people read the bible vertically they tend to take so long to read that by the time they read the next gospel they have forgotten most of what the previous gospel had said, so they don't catch the contradictions. As disturbing as it may be, something is very fishy concerning these biblical discrepancies.

There is no public record of the alleged crucifixion of Jesus even though the Romans kept public records of executions and crucifixions. It is alleged to have happened late Friday afternoon before the Sabbath started at sunset. Christians say Jews couldn't kill on the Sabbath, so that leaves little time to get the job done. However the Romans didn't observe the Sabbath and weren't Jewish, so they wouldn't have been in a rush or cared about violating the Sabbath. The standard policy for crucified persons was to leave the body on the cross for a long time until it was eaten by insects and completely decomposed. The Romans simply didn't care for alleged Jewish laws about the Sabbath and killed people on the Sabbath all the time, leaving crucified bodies on their crosses for weeks. The bible has a different version of crucifixion in which the gentile Romans are obeying alleged Jewish laws about the Sabbath for this one moment in history never done again before or after. Crucifixion is a very painful death by suffocation which occurs after the body loses the strength to stand upright and breathe, the longer it takes the more pain one endures. This is designed to take 3-5 days before death occurs, so it makes no sense that they would start the process with only hours left before the Sabbath if they planned on taking the bodies down, because nobody would've died in a few hours time, neither Jesus nor the thieves that were allegedly crucified next to him. Also in the Roman Empire theft was not a capital offense and thieves were not crucified. Only 3 types of people were ever sentenced to death by crucifixion in the Roman Empire, slaves, pirates and enemies of the state. So historically there shouldn't even be thieves alongside Jesus , yet mythologically it was in line with ancient tradition for a "sun of god" to be crucified along with thieves but we will discuss those myths later. Still realistically it would be illegal for the Roman soldiers to crucify the thieves the bible says were crucified. This would be like the U.S. government executing shoplifters via the electric chair. If the death of Jesus happened it would not have happened via crucifixion even if they broke the legs to speed up the process, keep in mind broken bones invalidates the sacrifice. So people say the guy on the cross was speared in the side as a reply. Although the thieves are not said to have been speared, apparently they did the impossible and died from crucifixion within hours although not having been flogged, scourged, or nailed. The bible mentions that Jesus was speared and liquid came out. Now let's assume it was blood, because we always hear that Christ shed his blood as payment for our sins thus Catholics claim they drink it. To shed blood means to cause blood to flow by cutting or wounding. A crown of thorns or scourging would not cause blood to flow, there would only be trickles, and typically shedding blood refers to killing, as in bloodshed. Blood is pumped by the heart and circulates the body as long as the heart keeps pumping. So if blood came out then it would mean that Jesus wasn't dead because the heart was still pumping blood out, if that's the case he didn't die on the cross and wasn't dead when/if speared. The only other liquid it could've been was water, if it was water and not blood that would mean that the heart had stopped pumping blood and the person was dead. However in that case no blood would've been shed. No matter how one looks at it, there is no way that Jesus could've died by crucifixion and shed blood, it's either one or the other but not both. For those who think being crucified or having nails pierce one's body constitutes shedding blood, this has been proven false by Pieter Van Debergh who himself was crucified in the way Christians say Jesus was with 4 inch nails driven through his hands and feet along with a 18 inch spike through his thigh for extra measure. He did not bleed the entire time, but more importantly he survived! Yes this guy was nailed to a cross in 1969 CE in front of witnesses who took pictures, in a more gruesome way than Christians say Jesus was crucified and he didn't bleed or die. Thus proving that timewise it is impossible for Jesus to have died via crucifixtion or to have shed his blood on a cross. This isn't an isolated incident either, in the Phillipines there is a annual tradition every "Good Friday" where fanatical Christians are voluntarily crucified with their hands nailed to a wooden cross with sterilized nails left to hang there because they want to experience what they think Jesus experienced. Some even use rusty nails instead of sterile, to be extra religious. None of them die and these acts are widely witnessed every year, sometimes these crucifixions are even broadcasted on television. Some of them even flagellate themselves. Not only do all survive but most aren't even tired afterwards, some people even smoke cigarettes after getting bandaged. Ruben Enaje has been nailed to a cross and crucified 33 times yet he survives until this day! Furthermore some of them claim they don't even feel pain because the "*spirit of Jesus gets inside and takes all the pain away because Christianity is true*". But then when the Shia flagellate themselves and cut their skulls open they say they feel no pain either because "*the spirit of Ali is in me and he takes all the pain away because Shiism is true*" with both deviant groups justifying falsehood with false logic. So the pain test is not a valid proof. Ironically by these Christians crucifying themselves the way they say Jesus was, they have proven that it would have been impossible for Jesus to have died via crucifiction in the timeframe the bible says. The authors of the gospels knew that their story was absurd so they specially included a verse in Mark 15:44, "44 *<u>Pilate was surprised to hear that he was already dead.</u> Summoning the centurion, <u>he asked him if Jesus had already died</u>*." That the bible says Pilate, who was an expert on crucifixions and allegedly sent Jesus to be crucified, was surprised to hear Jesus had died doesn't mean that Pilate actually heard this or did what is attributed to him. It only proves that even the gospel authors themselves knew that it was impossible for someone to die from crucifixion in such a short amount of time, even if they were scourged and nailed to the cross. Thus they inserted such a verse to make the surprising timeline of the story seem realistic and less suspicious. So in order for there to be any chance of them being believed they had to admit that it was unnatural for someone to die via crucifixion in less than 3 days. Yet still the Christian insists it had to be that Jesus was taken down before sunset because of the Sabbath and they say Jews couldn't kill on the Sabbath, which again if it was the Romans doing this as Christians say then they don't care and would leave him up. However lo and behold, unknown to Christians is that <u>Jews have no such law about not killing people on the Sabbath</u>, many people in the bible were killed on the Sabbath by Jews. Prophet Moses even allegedly stoned a guy to death on the Sabbath for carrying wood! So Jews killed people on the sabbath and the companions of Jesus knew this. It is a fact that <u>Jews can kill people on the Sabbath</u>, Christians made this law up to justify the story and explain the plot holes and impossibilities. But if the Romans kept bodies on crosses for days and Jews had no issue with killing on the sabbath, why then would anyone claim that Jesus had to be taken down specifically "before sunset". If the bible authors were making this up, why add such a implausible and blatantly false plot point? There was a specific reason why the story required Jesus to be taken down "before sunset". This was because of the snake cults. Snakes were thought to be able to get resurrected from the dead if their bodies were put back together "before sunset". So in order for snake cult members to believe Jesus to have been resurrected he had to have had his parts put back together "before sunset". Now of course the bible doesn't say he "had his parts put back together" but that he was allegedly taken down "before sunset" was enough for the snake cultists to be satisfied, as an extra bonus his knees were broken so he couldn't walk just like a snake can't walk. Likewise he was speared just as the "Caliostro" snake symbol was impaled by an arrow which saved the world from the dangers of the apple of knowledge just as Christians would come to believe the spearing of Jesus forgave the dangers of the Original Sin allegedly gotten from Adam and Eve because they ate a forbidden fruit which Christians then said was an apple. They even put a snake-cult favorite verse in the New Testament in John 3:14 which claims *"Just as Moses lifted up the snake in the wilderness, so the Son of Man must be lifted up"* to which most Christians incorrectly correlate this verse to the idolatrous snake idol Nehushtan which the bible falsely attributes to Moses creating, initially as a way to heal snake bites just by looking at the snake image; despite his 2nd commandment being a forbiddance of graven images.

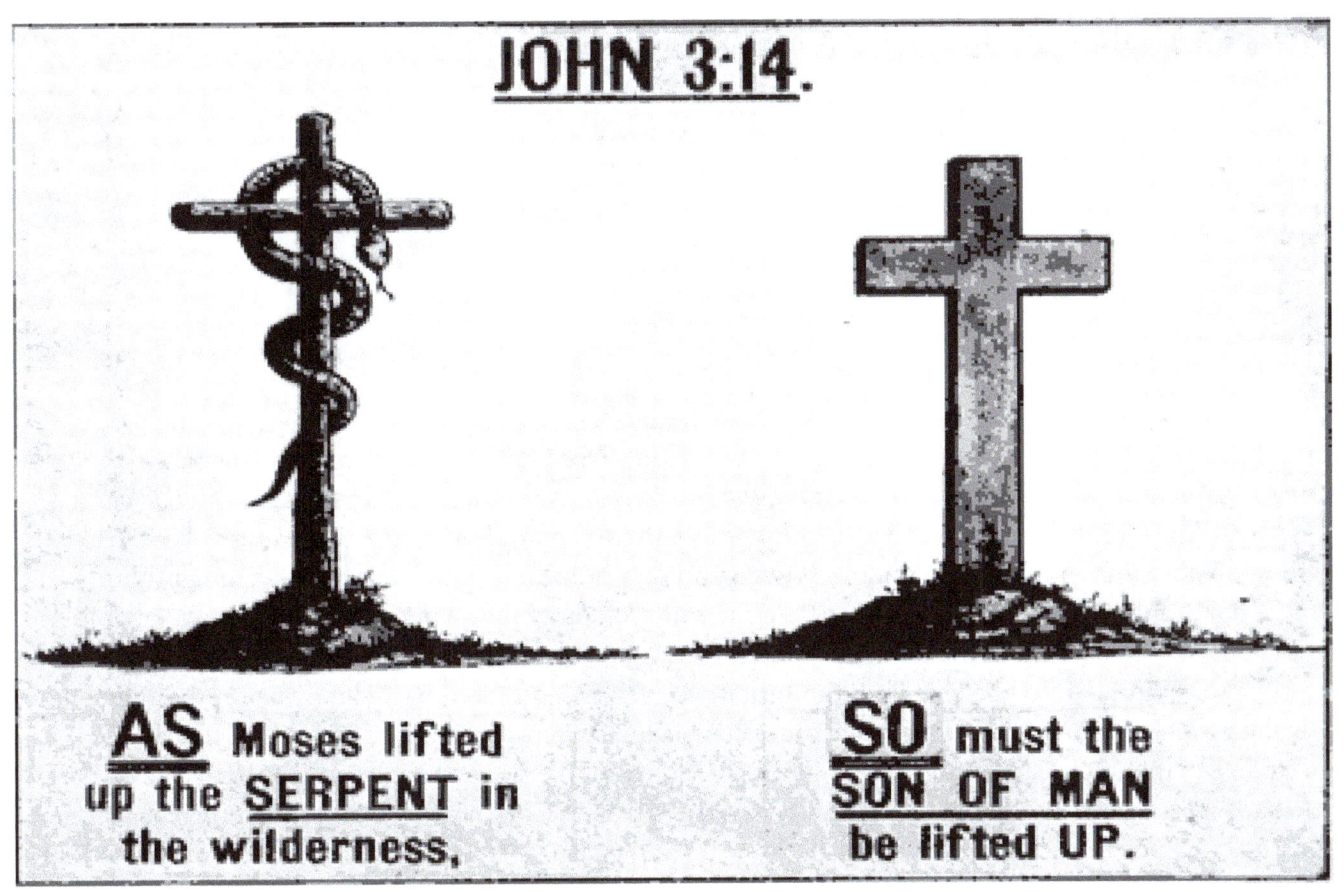

Originally John 3:14 use to mean that just as Moses picked up the serpent and it became his staff so must people(son of man, meaning humans) trust in a seemingly dangerous yet strong uplifting faith to achieve success in paradise. However as faith in the crucifiction story grew and was preached to snake cult members this verse meaning was distorted and linked to a snake idol that the Israelite King Hezekiah biblically destroyed due to it being worshipped as a god but because the same bibles attribute a bronze snake effigy on a stick to Moses, in the book of Numbers, as a miraculous snake bite cure the Christians then contend that Jesus on a cross is just like the snake statue on a cross/stick and that became the crux of their faith which they portend was biblically foreshadowed. Despite the verse of John 3:13 plainly saying the Old Testament verses and other New Testament verses were false when it said Elijah and Enoch went to heaven. The bible verses which contradict John 3:13 are below:

2 Kings 2:11

*"As they were walking along and talking together, suddenly a chariot of fire and horses of fire appeared and separated the two of them, and **Elijah went up to heaven** in a whirlwind."*

Hebrews 11:5

*By faith **Enoch** was taken from this life, so that **he did not experience death**: "He could not be found, because **God had taken him away.**" For before he was taken, he was commended as one who pleased God.*

So the scholastic reader would have chronologically first read these Old Testament verses long before they read John 3:13 which says *"No one has ever gone into heaven except the one who came from heaven – the Son of Man."* before they ever knew of the verses John 3:16 or John 3:14 and then would've stopped reading at John 3:13 because they'd know that John's information is flawed and contradicts the Old Testament writings about several of God's prophets going to heaven. Thus we can only conclude that whoever wrote the gospel of John didn't know what the bible said in the Old Testament or the New Testament. Or the author of John did know what the bible said but he didn't believe in it, thought it was wrong and thought he knew better than the bible. It really is the gospel of John vs. the bible. One must be rejected because they cannot reconcile. Or did God inspire John to say the other part of the bible is wrong? Thus if John 3:13 is wrong then John 3:16 cannot be accepted. Sadly it's even worse than I described, because the reason Christians like to quote John 3:16 so much is because the bible portrays Jesus as the speaker. Well the bible also says Jesus is the one who said what John 3:13 says. So all that stuff I said about John 3:13 being wrong, that's not quite the full story. Because it's not just John but the Jesus whom John writes about. Thus we must really have an answer to the question of who is wrong? The Old Testament or John's version of Jesus? If John's version of Jesus is the real version then it would mean Jesus is wrong or made a mistake when publicly preaching and prophets never make public preaching errors. So if John's gospel account is wrong then that means the Jesus written about in John is not the true Jesus. Also Jesus is famous for having taught in parables but the gospel of John has zero parables attributed to Jesus. According to the gospel of John, Jesus didn't use parables. It seems to me whoever wrote John's gospel didn't know Jesus. Paul had never met Jesus during his time on earth yet 52% of the New Testament is allegedly written by Paul. Luke acted as Paul's physician and likewise had never actually met or heard Jesus during his time on earth. The Gospel of Luke 1:1-4 even has the author stating:

"*Many have undertaken to draw up an account* of the things that have been fulfilled among us, ² *just as they were handed down to us* by those who from the first were eyewitnesses and servants of the word.³ **With this in mind**, since I myself have carefully investigated everything from the beginning, *I too decided to write* an orderly account for you, most excellent **Theophilus**,⁴ *so that you may know the certainty of the things you have been taught*."

The problem is that the "Theophilus" whom Luke addressed this to was bishop of Antioch from 169-177 CE. This means the earliest Luke's gospel could've been written was 169 CE. It could not possibly have been Luke the alleged companion of Jesus who actually wrote it unless he lived to be over 150 years old. But then why wait over 130 years before writing down the life of Jesus? Was he waiting for a special type of ink to be invented or what? The Catholic Encyclopedia says that the gospel of Luke was not written until 200 years after the events it describes. According to the Catholic Encyclopedia, at the time he allegedly wrote the gospel Luke was over 200 years old! Don't you think he would have been a little more famous had that been the case? After all how many authors can claim to have been over 200 years old before they started writing? Also the very author of the gospel writes that he wasn't eyewitness to the events he is writing about and that he has read the writings of other people. What he was writing was not the word of God, or inspired by God in his eyes. The author himself says he wrote stuff based on what others wrote in order to support what has already been taught and believed in. The "scripture" was written after the belief was taught, so the belief created the writings instead of the writings creating the belief. This is understood when we see the author of John clearly telling falsehoods or else the Old Testament is telling multiple falsehoods because of this contradiction in the bible. A sincere person couldn't base their faith on the very next verse John 3:14 that is next to a verse that contradicts known facts about previous prophets going to heaven. Basically John 3:13 says the Old Testament is false in multiple spots and then John 3:14 is used by Christians to say "See the Old Testament predicts the crucifixion!" thus they believe it is prophesied truth. However most Christians never ever read John 3:13 but only get other pro-Christian pieces of the bible preached to them so they don't see the contradictions and plot holes. We will discuss the snake cult beliefs which existed prior to Christianity later after showing the biblical contradictions regarding the crucifixion amongst the 4 gospels written about Jesus which were never written or read or approved by Jesus himself. The reason different gospels exist in the New Testament is because the different gospel authors thought the other gospels contained incorrect information that disagreed with what they personally believed, so they wrote their own gospel to fix the errors of the other gospels. Yet their gospel was suspected of containing incorrect information as well, so they only added to the confusion and amount of incorrect information. Likewise Christians have different editions and versions of the bible for the same reason, because the other bibles don't say what they believe in so they make a bible that does. The existence of multiple gospels shows that none of the gospel authors considered the other authors to be divinely inspired. Nor did they claim or think they were writing down divine revelation themselves. The gospels were written by Christians to support their own beliefs, none of the gospels in the bible say they are written by or inspired by God.

      To justify the impossibility of death by crucifixtion in such a short time for the non-snake cult converts the lie about Jewish Sabbath laws was told and of course the pagan converts to Christianity wouldn't know any better, just as the Christians today don't know better because they don't research Judaism to see if what they get told about it by Christians is actually true. Nobody has ever believed in what Christians say that the Jews have always believed in, you can ask the Jews themselves to verify this but Christians tend not to listen or even hear the truth of it. Instead Christians think that the Jews all have and always have believed in the Christian fantasy of what they say Judaism is. Also when people were crucified in the Roman Empire they were naked, no loincloths were used and God, a son of God, or a prophet of God would never ever be humiliated in such a filthy fashion on a cross for all to gawk at in the nude. If Jesus were crucified he would have been completely naked with his circumcised penis seen by everybody as well as the testicles. This is beyond shameful for a prophet of God to endure, even more so for a "son of God", or God himself. Would God let everyone jeer at his prophet's nude crotch? Christians unwittingly claim God sent Jesus as a naked sacrifice. Inform them that any who saw this happen would've seen and been able to measure the size of Jesus' penis. So how big was it? That's an important detail they never mention or imagine. But Christians actually teach that God desired a naked Jesus to get whipped, crowned, stripped, carry some wood, then get nailed on a piece of wood, which was then erected with him bleeding out while asphyxiating for us to get eternal bliss. Some perverts might say that's a sadistic erotic sexually symbolic ritual. The climax is said to be when he got speared and a bunch of bodily fluids gushed forth. Oh I almost forgot, Christans say these bodily fluids were shed intentionally for us to drink. It almost sounds like a pornographic movie plot. Gives a whole different meaning to the Christian slogan of "Jesus loves you". Or P.P. (Pontius Pilate) "washing his hands" of the matter. Whereas if the crucifixes were accurately historically depicted, it'd be a naked Jesus including his penis and testicles on the most famous pornographic pendant ever. Almost like a pagan phallic idol. Thus if Christians insist on sinfully depicting Jesus on a cross they should show us the penis and testicles too. If they don't then they shouldn't make any pictures or movies of it at all. We want the truth, the bare naked truth about Jesus! Speaking of the truth, where's the poop? Jesus is said to have had a large "last supper" with food and drink. Nearly 24 hours later he allegedly dies on a cross. Now when you are crucified they don't let you take bathroom breaks. People who were crucified would be naked and during the days it took to die they would poop and pee right where they were hung. So just imagine Jesus up on the cross, naked and urinating. Also sometimes when humans die their body expels feces and urine. It doesn't happen all the time but it does happen when people die in a hanging position because of the suspension effect. So if naked Jesus died on the cross, he would've pooped on the cross too. Crap would be on that cross if Jesus died on it. Neither God nor Jesus is ashamed of the truth so if Christians are ashamed to show the world a naked Jesus crucified pissing on the crowd and pooping on the cross, then maybe it means their pictures and doctrines could be filthy lies. The truth is beautiful, if Jesus died naked for my sins that'd be a beautiful thing to see. Why then does it feel so disgusting?

    The bible mentions after the alleged crucifixion that Jesus was placed in a sepulchre. Consider the circumstances, the Jews and Romans hate this person and just executed him, the Jews say he's heretical and the Romans that he's an enemy of the state. Typically when people were crucified they were criminals and buried in unmarked lots with the other criminals in mass graves, that is if there was anything left to bury that didn't decompose before they took the corpse down. Although the bible says that this heretical enemy of the state was put into a special burial place. There is no way a heretic would be given such a privilege and no government would allow for an enemy of the state to be honored after execution. For example Che Guevara and Osama bin Laden have unknown graves so their followers couldn't make their grave into a shrine, rallying point or symbol. Obviously Jesus or his followers couldn't afford a fancy place so the bible says it was generously donated. In the eyes of the authorities Jesus was a cult leader and they soon began persecuting his followers after his departure. Who in their right mind would say to the roman government, "*Can I have the body of that guy everyone hates and you just killed for being an enemy to the state, so that I can put his body in a special dignified place?*" Also keep in mind the guy is not said to have been related, he'd be in a difficult position to explain his affection for someone who had the same stigma an executed terrorist has today. If the government gave up this crucified person's body then they would've set a precedent and every person who got crucified after that would have their family and friends asking for the body so they could bury it the way they wanted, historically this did not happen and no precedent for it was ever set. The gospel of John 19:39 describes 75 pounds of myrrh being put on the body in the sepulchre, 75 pounds! Myrrh was the perfume of the kings, used on Egyptian mummies and allegedly given to Jesus as a baby by a King who visited his manger. Perfume was expensive at that time given that according to the gospel of John a pint (or 16 ounces/a pound) of perfume would cost a year's worth of a servant's wages. Meaning an average Jewish person would need 75 years worth of wages to buy "expensive perfume" whereas myrrh was the perfume used by Kings so that's a royal price to pay. Yet this very same gospel of John that says 75 pounds of myrrh were brought by Nicomedus even though it also says in John 12:7 that Jesus himself said to a person in putting a pint of perfume on him 6 days before Passover that they had done so to prepare him for his burial. So John's Jesus says he's had enough perfume in chapter 12, but then John says Nicodemus was bringing 75 pounds of the royal perfume to put on Jesus before his burial 7 chapters later. Yet Matthew, Luke and Mark also mention Jesus getting perfumed 3 different ways all 2 days before the Passover. So Jesus said once was enough, but biblically he got it 4 different ways on separate days and then gets 75 more pounds. Seriously that has to be a world record amount of perfume. Also did they think nobody would smell 75 pounds of perfume being transported or poured all in one location? I can't even have a drop of perfume on me or even carry a milliliter of perfume closed in a sealed container without my parents angrily complaining that I'm stinking up everything. I don't even know if perfume shops today carry 75 pounds of perfume total. 75 pounds of perfume might even be a biohazardous danger to smell or pour on one individual. 75 pounds of perfume could possibly even dissolve a dead body entirely, or even a living body. But what would Jesus want? I guess these followers of Jesus thought buying 75 pounds of the royal perfume used by kings for Jesus who already said he'd had enough perfume for burial was the best use of their money instead of giving to the poor as Jesus taught them to do. Accounting for scarcity and economic conditions, this perfume could easily have cost over 100 years worth of an average person's wages. I guess they thought the ascetic Jesus really wanted them to perfume him and break / make a world record in the process. But only the gospel of John has this story. Since John was the latest of the 4 canonical gospels to be written, it is suspicious that the other gospels forgot the 75 pounds of perfume, seems like something one wouldn't forget seeing as it'd be so expensive. However if you were a pagan Egyptian accustomed to the god-like Pharaohs thought to be the divine sons of the gods being elaborately mummified, then to believe in Jesus being a son of a god or a god who died then you would need to expect such a royal extravagent smelly burial service. Thus it got written up in John and John alone, in a way that would make Egyptians proud and synchronize with their beliefs. On Sunday the bible has Mary Magdalene going to the sepulchre to anoint Jesus, when you anoint someone it basically means you wash their head. Now why would a female follower of an enemy of the state be going out all alone so soon after her leader had been executed while all the men are hiding inside as wanted criminals? Or at least John and Mark say she was alone, Matthew says she was with other women. So in the bible we have 2 gospels saying she was alone, 1 says she wasn't. Again both can't be right. She was either alone or not, or neither.

    In reference to when "Jesus" was captured Mark 14:50-52 say: "[50] *Then everyone deserted him and fled.*[51] *A young man, wearing nothing but a linen garment, was following Jesus. When they seized him,* [52] *he fled naked, leaving his garment behind.*" These verses show just how terrified the companions of Jesus were, afraid for their own lives and the coming crackdown. Now *everyone* means everyone. This biblical verse itself says that no one was there to witness what happened after Jesus was taken, no one saw or heard what actually happened when Jesus was said to have been taken and sentenced and they are not mentioned as being present at the alleged crucifixion either. However people will maintain that the story of what happened was divinely inspired to the authors, God knows best. It is important to remember that according to the bible everyone left Jesus and there were no eyes or ears to witness what really happened if and when he was captured by the authorities. The bible says Mark, Matthew, Luke and John weren't there. Yet I showed the above verses in Mark to a Christian, and he asked me if I knew who that "young man" who ran was and I replied in the negative. So he told me it was Mark, which I can see how he'd think that since if none but Jesus and the young man following were left then the only 2 who would know about the guy running naked when seized would be either Jesus, the young man or those who tried to seize him. Thus since Mark is the alleged author, logically by process of elimination one would assume it was Mark and he didn't write in the first person or say it was him because he was embarrassed. I mean afterall who'd want to write that they were such a coward they ran away naked ditching Jesus? Yet there is a problem with this scandalous action being blamed on Mark. This is because Matthew and Luke list Peter as being the only one who followed behind Jesus when he was arrested. Other Christians say it was John since he was supposedly the youngest of them all. Others say since John was the youngest and it was written in Mark then that's a clue it was "John Mark" who is a different guy than both Mark and John. Others say the term "linen garment" indicates it was a burial shroud and since they were in a place used by Jews to bury their dead then because Jesus identified himself as "I am he" when arrested, according to the gospel of John, afterwhich people drew back and fell to the ground, then it must've been a sonic boom/declaration that Jesus was God which resulted in a dead young man coming back to life who stumbled into the crowd and fled naked when they tried to seize him. So all these different Christians say the biblical truth is that it was Mark, John, Peter, John Mark, a dead young guy who was resurrected via the sonic boom of Jesus' voice , and there are probably some other theories that I'm not aware of. While the bible says what the bible says, what it means depends on who you ask. Yet they all agree the bible is true, for the most part, they just disagree on what exactly that "biblical truth" is, although if you don't believe in their "biblical truth" then you are a disbeliever. Trust me I know, they all think I'm a disbeliever. They all agree one must absolutely believe in the bible or else, but just don't ask them what exactly the bible means. If you do ask them they say that you have to believe what they believe it means or else you don't really believe in the bible at all. Yet why don't they just say from the start that the true belief one has to have just so happens to be what they believe the bible means? This is why Christians tend not to read the bible, since being a Christian isn't really about believing in the bible.

Christianity is really about believing a particular interpretation of the bible, or else. So it's not about the bible persay, it's about what people say. Most feel little need to read as long as they feel they believe. Afterall prophet Jesus didn't read the bible, so why should they?

So Mary Magdalene is going to the sepulchre to anoint Jesus , why in the world would she be going to wash the head of a dead body? Rigimortis sets in 3 hours after death, meaning if you wash the head of a dead rotting body 3 days after death the body would fall apart, and no Jew, Christian or Muslim does this practice of washing the dead body days after it's been laid to rest. Why would she do that to a dead entombed person? Did she think Jesus was alive? Then when she arrives the place is empty and the body isn't found, keep in mind this alleged place was on the property of the rich man who donated the sepulchre, near his house and farm where gardeners and farmers would be working growing wheat and such. The following text is not a direct quote from the bible rather it is conflated from different bible verses from different gospels. Christians often do this when piecing together the Easter story because if they read one gospel alone it would read much different than picking and choosing bits from each and combining them. These excerpts are from "*The Desire of Ages*" by the Christian evangelist Ellen G. White but most of the dialogue is from John 20:11-17. Ellen just removed some bits from John and added extra stuff from the other gospels concerning Mary Magdalene learning what happened to Jesus : "*thinking that she must find someone who could tell her what had been done with the body of Jesus. Another voice addressed her, "Woman, why weepest thou? whom seekest thou?" Through her tear-dimmed eyes, Mary __saw the form of a man, and thinking that it was the gardener__, she said, "Sir, if thou have borne Him hence, tell me where thou hast laid Him, and __I will take Him away__*."

Mary Magdalene thinks it's the gardener she is speaking to and Ellen G. White says Mary said she would "*take Him away*" referring to Jesus. Realistically if Jesus were dead there is no way 1 woman could carry a rotting dead body all by herself that is likely over 150 pounds, so what did she mean? Did she really think a gardener would have moved a dead stinking body somewhere else without telling the property owner about the body found on the property? Why would she think Jesus to be a gardener? Was he wearing gardener clothes as a disguise? Ellen G. White continues: "*But now in His own familiar voice Jesus said to her, "Mary." Now she knew that it was not a stranger who was addressing her, and turning she saw before her __the living Christ__. __In her joy she forgot that He had been crucified.__ Springing toward Him, as if to embrace His feet, she said, "Rabboni." But Christ raised His hand, saying, Detain Me not; "for I am not yet ascended to My Father: but go to My brethren, and say unto them, I ascend unto __My Father, and your Father__; and __to My God, and your God__.*" *And Mary went her way to the disciples with the joyful message.*" Now she recognizes him as the "*living Christ*" not the risen Christ, but the living. "*In her joy she forgot that He had been crucified*" how could she forget he had been crucified but not forget he had died? Had she thought she was going to visit a dead body she would have forgotten he had died, but instead it says she forgot he was crucified. You don't forget the method a person died in but remember that they're dead, especially if you care so much that you were going to visit their place of burial. If we read between the lines then it would seem as though Jesus did not die and had survived the ordeal. The miracle is not that Jesus is risen but that he is still living, which is the sign of Jonah promised in the gospel of Matthew. He looked like a human and wasn't in spirit form. She was coming to anoint him, Christ means anointed one. She offered to take him away by herself. She calls him Rabboni, meaning teacher, not God, or the son of God, or Lord, or Lamb of God, or savior; all of this indicates that she didn't think he was dead, risen or divine. A sepulchre itself is not a tomb or grave but a chamber, not necessarily used for dead people. Mary started to weep only after she saw the sepulchre was empty. If you were going to see a dead body in a coffin and found it empty you wouldn't start crying, you'd be concerned what happened to it or think you were at the wrong place. Although if you were going to tend to a living injured man who has many enemies and found him not to be there, you would cry thinking his enemies had captured him and you had been too late to stop them or help the injured man. It is also significant Ellen G. White uses the bit from John which has Jesus saying "*My God, and your God*", this is after the alleged resurrection and still Jesus is not saying he is God, but is using inclusive language referring to himself as having the same relationship to God as other humans. While the timing still doesn't add up, if Jesus had survived it would be easier to say he made good on his promise to the Pharisees that they would get a miracle like that of Jonah. Perhaps Jesus was crucified and stayed alive? I do not believe Jesus was killed nor crucified and have good reasons for thinking so, I just mention these alternate theories just to be fair and demonstrate how Christians don't even agree that Jesus died or when and how he was allegedly crucified. In the 3rd century CE there were more than 25 different stories of how the alleged crucifixion, death and resurrection happened. Since then many have been discounted as false despite people having lived and died believing them to be true. Some even thought Jesus survived crucifixion and lived out his days in Egypt or India dying a natural death, but these are false versions too.

Now let us finally see what the alleged biblical witnesses (gospels) have to say about the crucifiction and cross examine them in a table to make sure they aren't telling any lies or contradicting each other, since they should all be describing the same event. Any shady stories contradicting the other witnesses (gospels) will be shaded in a different color to distinguish it. If they all agree then each row in the table will be the same solid color.

	Matthew	*Mark*	*Luke*	*John*
Did Judas Kiss Jesus ?	<u>**YES**</u> ⁴⁸ *Now the betrayer had arranged a signal with them:* <u>*"The one I kiss is the man; arrest him."*</u> ⁴⁹ *Going at once to Jesus,* <u>*Judas said,*</u> <u>*"Greetings, Rabbi!"*</u> *and* <u>*kissed him.*</u> <u>*Jesus replied, "Do what you came for, friend."*</u> *Then the men stepped forward, seized Jesus and arrested him* (26:48-50)	<u>**YES**</u>*, but in a different way* ⁴⁴ *Now the betrayer had arranged a signal with them:* <u>*"The one I kiss is the man; arrest him*</u> *and* <u>*lead him away under guard."*</u> ⁴⁵ *Going at once to Jesus,* <u>*Judas said, "Rabbi!" and kissed him.*</u> (14:44-45)	<u>No, but he tried to do so</u> *While he was still speaking a crowd came up, and the man who was called Judas, one of the Twelve, was leading them.* <u>*He approached Jesus to kiss him,*</u> ⁴⁸ *but Jesus asked him,* <u>*"Judas, are you betraying the Son of Man with a kiss?"*</u> (22:47-48)	<u>**NO**, he didn't plan or try to</u> ³ *So* <u>*Judas came*</u> *to the* <u>*garden, guiding a detachment of soldiers and some officials from the chief priests and the Pharisees. They were carrying torches, lanterns and weapons.*</u> ⁴ *Jesus, knowing all that was going to happen to him, went out and asked them,* <u>*"Who is it you want?"*</u> ⁵ <u>*"Jesus of Nazareth," they replied. "I am he," Jesus said. (And Judas the traitor was standing there with them.)*</u> ⁶ *When* <u>*Jesus said, "I am he,"*</u> *they drew back and fell to the ground.* ⁷ *Again he asked them, "Who is it you want?" "Jesus of Nazareth," they said.* ⁸ *Jesus answered, "I told you that I am he. If you are*

				looking for me, then let these men go."
				(18:3-8)
What happened after the betrayal and the arrest? Was there a swordfight? If so who fought who and what happened? Also what did Jesus have to say about any such swordfight? Did Jesus perform any miracles	⁵¹ With that, **one of Jesus' companions reached for his sword, drew it out and struck the servant of the high priest, cutting off his ear.** ⁵² **"Put your sword back in its place," Jesus said to him, "for all who draw the sword will die by the sword.** ⁵³ Do you think I cannot call on my Father, and he will at once put at my disposal more than twelve legions of angels?(⁵⁴ But how then would the Scriptures be fulfilled that say it must happen in this way?" ⁵⁵ In that hour **Jesus said to the crowd, "Am I leading a**	The men seized Jesus and arrested him. ⁴⁷ **Then one of those standing near drew his sword and struck the servant of the high priest, cutting off his ear.** ⁴⁸ **"Am I leading a rebellion," said Jesus, "that you have come out with swords and clubs to capture me? ⁴⁹ Every day I was with you, teaching in the temple courts, and you did not arrest me. But the Scriptures must be fulfilled."** ⁵⁰ Then everyone deserted him and fled. ⁵¹ **A young man, wearing nothing but a linen garment, was following**	When Jesus' followers saw what was going to happen, **they said, "Lord, should we strike with our swords?" ⁵⁰ And one of them struck the servant of the high priest, cutting off his right ear.⁵¹ But Jesus answered, "No more of this!" And he touched the man's ear and healed him.** ⁵² Then Jesus said to the chief priests, the officers of the temple guard, and the elders, who had come for him, **"Am I leading a rebellion, that you have come with swords and clubs? ⁵³ Every day I was with you in the temple courts, and**	This happened so that the words he had spoken would be fulfilled: "I have not lost one of those you gave me." ¹⁰ Then **Simon Peter, who had a sword, drew it and struck the high priest's servant, cutting off his right ear. (The servant's name was Malchus.)** ¹¹ **Jesus commanded Peter, "Put your sword away! Shall I not drink the cup the Father has given me?"** ¹² Then **the detachment of soldiers with its commander and the Jewish officials arrested Jesus.** They bound him ¹³ and brought him first to Annas, who was the father-in-law of Caiaphas, the high priest that year. ¹⁴ Caiaphas was

when getting arrested?	*rebellion, that you have come out with swords and clubs to capture me? Every day I sat in the temple courts teaching, and you did not arrest me.* ⁵⁶ *But this has all taken place that the writings of the prophets might be fulfilled." Then all the disciples deserted him and fled.* Those who had arrested Jesus took him to Caiaphas the high priest, where the teachers of the law and the elders had assembled. ⁵⁸ But **Peter followed him at a distance, *right up to the courtyard*** of the high priest. **He entered and sat down with the guards to** see the outcome. (26:51-58)	*Jesus. When they seized him,* ⁵² *he fled naked, leaving his garment behind.* ⁵³ *They took Jesus to the high priest, and all the chief priests, the elders and the teachers of the law came together.* ⁵⁴ *Peter followed him at a distance, right into the courtyard of the high priest. There he sat with the guards and warmed himself at the fire.* (14:46-54) Note the swordfighters are unnamed, Jesus says nothing about bad swordfighting, he only says Scripture must be fulfilled without any specifice way. No miracle occurs, No angels are mentioned. A man is mentioned	*you did not lay a hand on me. But this is your hour— when darkness reigns."* ⁵⁴ *Then seizing him, they led him away and took him into the house of the high priest.* **Peter followed at a distance.** ⁵⁵ *And when* **some there had kindled a fire in the middle of the courtyard** *and had sat down together,* **Peter sat down with them.** (22:49-53) Note that Jesus is asked permission to fight with swords then after a "right ear" gets cut off by an unnamed swordfighter Jesus says that's enough fighting and miraculously heals	the one who had advised the Jewish leaders that it would be good if one man died for the people. ¹⁵ **Simon Peter and another disciple were following Jesus.** Because **this disciple was known to the high priest, he went with Jesus into the high priest's courtyard,** ¹⁶ **but Peter had to wait outside at the door.** The other disciple, who was known to the high priest, came back, spoke to the servant girl on duty there and brought Peter in. ¹⁷ "You aren't one of this man's disciples too, are you?" she asked Peter. He replied, "I am not." ¹⁸ It was cold, and the **servants and officials stood around a fire** they had made to keep warm. **Peter also was standing with them,** warming himself.

	Note the swordfighters are unnamed, Jesus says not to swordfight, and Scripture must be fulfilled specifically this way, no miracle occurs and Peter goes UP TO the courtyard and <u>voluntarily sits with the guards who arrested Jesus</u>.	following Jesus but flees naked when the guards attempted to seize him, it is possibly the same guy who did the swordfight. Peter goes INTO the courtyard and <u>voluntarily sits with the guards who arrested Jesus by a fire to get warm.</u>	the wounded. Swordfight was done with Jesus' permission and he simply said enough was enough. Nothing is mentioned about Scripture or angels and Peter <u>sits</u> IN THE MIDDLE of the courtyard <u>with regular folk at a fire</u>.	*(18:9-18)* Note Peter is named as the swordfighter who cut off a "right ear", Jesus stops the fight but performs no miracle at all. No angels or Scriptures are mentioned but the words of Jesus are mentioned as fulfilled as well as a cup. Then Jesus is taken to Anas before going to court. <u>Peter and another follow</u>, whereas <u>Peter isn"t allowed to enter the courtyard.</u> Peter only gets in when the other disciple negotiates his entry and Peter denies Jesus. Then he voluntarily <u>STANDS</u> with the officials who witnessed the arrest and him cutting off a soldier's ear.

Was Jesus blindfolded and spit on?	**Not blindfolded but spit on** *Then they spit in his face and struck him with their fists. Others slapped him (26:67)*	*Yes Then some began to spit at him; they blindfolded him, struck him with their fists, and said, "Prophesy!" And the guards took him and beat him. (14:65)*	*Yes <u>without spitting</u> but with test question pertaining to blindfolding* *They blindfolded him and demanded, "Prophesy! Who hit you?" (22:64)*	Not mentioned
Did Jesus get sent to Herod and did Pilate's wife intercede?	**No/Yes** he only saw Pilate and Pilate's wife intercedes(27:19)	**No/No** he only saw Pilate with **no mention of Pilate's wife's dream or intercession**	*Yes/No* he went to both Herod and Pilate *(23:7-16)* but there is no mention of Pilate's wife	**No/No** There is no mention of Herod and no mention of Pilate's wife despite seeing Pilate.
Was Jesus flogged by Pilate?	**Yes flogged but with unique dialogue found only in Matthew different from the rest of the versions**	**Yes flogged but with unique dialogue found only in Mark different from the rest of the versions**	**Not flogged but "punished" with unique dialogue only in Luke different from the rest of the versions**	**Yes flogged but Pilate talks to him 2 separate times, even after he had him flogged, with unique dialogue not found elsewhere.**
What was Jesus wearing?	<u>***They stripped him and put a scarlet robe on him,***</u> *(27:28)*	<u>***They put a purple robe on him***</u>*, then twisted together a crown of thorns and set it on him. (15:17)*	Not mentioned	*The soldiers twisted together a crown of thorns and put it on his head.* <u>***They clothed him in a purple robe***</u> *(19:2)(In the Greek, John's purple is a different purple than Mark's color)*

Who carried the cross?	**Simon** of Cyrene (27:32)	**Simon** of Cyrene, the father of Alexander and Rufus (15:21)	**Simon** of Cyrene (23:26)	**Only Jesus** (19:17)
What time was Jesus () crucified?	**3:00 PM** (27:46)	**9:00 AM** (15:25)	Not mentioned	**12:00 PM** (19:14-15)
Which day was Jesus () crucified?	The first day of Passover, the **15th of Nissan** (26:17-25)	The first day of Passover the **15th day of Nissan** (14:12-21)	The first day of Passover **15th day of Nissan** (22:7-18)	The day before Passover, **14th day of Nissan** (13:1,29, 18:28, 19:14)
What did the sign on the cross say?	*Above his head they placed the written charge against him:* <u>*this is jesus, the king of the jews.*</u> (27:37)	*The written notice of the charge against him read:* <u>*the king of the jews.*</u> (15:26)	*There was a written notice above him, which read:* <u>*this is the king of the jews.*</u> (23:38)	*Pilate had a notice prepared and fastened to the cross. It read:* <u>*jesus of nazareth, the king of the jews.*</u> (19:19)
How did the other 2 being crucified treat Jesus?	Both "rebels" remain silent, as does Jesus. The crowd mocks making allegations which include blasphemy to which Jesus makes no comment when asked to prove the blasphemous claims he's accused of. (27:38-44)	Both "rebels" remain silent, as does Jesus. The crowd mocks making nearly identical allegations as in Matthew except without the accusations of blasphemy. (15:27-32)	There are 2 "criminals" 1 taunts, the other 1 rebukes the taunter. The 2nd "criminal", who calls Jesus a man, is promised paradise by Jesus despite the 2nd criminal not believing in Christian doctrines. (23:39-43)	Not mentioned

Did Jesus drink?	Took 1 sip then refused	No	Not mentioned	He "*received the drink*"
What was the drink?	Wine mixed with gall (27:34)(Pagan belief was that drinking gall would result in a curse, or cause madness.)	Jesus is offered wine mixed with myrrh (15:23)	Vinegar (sour wine) (23:36)	Vinegar (sour wine) (19:29-30)
What were the last words of Jesus on the cross?	"**Eli, Eli**, lema sabachthani" translated as "My God, my God, why have you forsaken me?" (27:46)	"**Eloi,Eloi**, lema sabachthani"translated as "My God, my God, why have you forsaken me?" (15:34)	"Father, into your hands I commit my spirit." (23: 46)	"*It is finished*" (19:30)
When and who prepared the spices?	Not mentioned	**Mary purchased** the spices **after** the Sabbath was over. (16:1)	**Mary made** the spices at home **before** the Sabbath started. (23:56)	*Nicodemus, **prepared 75 pounds of spices** **before** the Sabbath, later bringing them to the sepulchre.* (19:39)
Had the sun risen when the women came to the tomb?	It was **toward dawn** the first day of the week. (28:1)	**YES** They came to the tomb **after sunrise**. (16:2)	At **early dawn** they went to the tomb. (24:1)	**NO** Mary came early to the tomb, while it was **still dark.** (20:1)
How many days and how many nights	**3 days** and 2 nights (28:1)	**3 days** and 2 nights (16:2)	**3 days** and 2 nights (24:1)	**2 days** and 2 nights (20:1) *It was still dark at night, so at max only 2*

was Jesus in the tomb?				*less than full days can count.*
How many came to the tomb and who?	**TWO** Mary and Mary Magdalene (28:1)	*THREE Salome, Mary Magdalene and Mary the mother of James (16:1)*	**MORE** than **FOUR** Mary Magdalene, Mary the mother of James, Joanna, and other women (24:10)	**ONE** Only Mary Magdalene (20:1)
Was the stone already removed when the women arrived?	**No** After the women arrive <u>an earthquake occurs before they see an angel roll back the stone and sit on it</u> (28:1-2)	**Yes** Upon arrival they were <u>surprised to find the stone was already rolled away</u>. **No angel or earthquake** mentioned at all. (16:3-4)	**Yes** When they arrived <u>the stone had already been taken away</u>. **No angel or earthquake** mentioned at all. (24:2)	**Yes** When Mary arrived, <u>the stone had already been taken away</u>. **No angel or earthquake** mentioned at all. (20:1)
How many angels were at the tomb? What were they doing at the scene? Where were they?	One Angel <u>Sitting</u> (28:2) On the stone he rolled away from the tomb	One young man <u>Sitting</u> (16:5) On the right side inside the tomb	Two men <u>Standing</u> (24:4) By them, inside the tomb	<u>**Nobody**</u> when Mary comes to the tomb. <u>When Mary arrives a second time she finds</u> **two angels** sitting: one at the head and one at the feet. (20:1-2,12)
What do the angels or men tell the visitors to do?	"go *quickly* and <u>**tell his disciples**</u>: *'He has risen from the dead and is going **ahead of***	" go <u>**tell his disciples and Peter**</u> *he is going **before you to Galilee**!"* (16:6-7)	No instructions are given at all they simply leave and return. Later telling the apostles and	<u>**No instructions**</u> the angels only ask "<u>*Why are you weeping woman?*</u>" when Mary turns around she sees

	you into Galilee." (28:7)		others what they did and saw that day but nobody believed them. (24:9-11)	Jesus standing there and he gives her instructions, not angels. (20:13-17)
Do the tomb visitors even tell the disciples about their experience?	**Yes** they *"ran to tell his disciples"* (28:8)	**No** *"they said nothing to anyone; for they were afraid."* (16:8)	**Yes** *"Returning from the tomb, they told all this to the eleven..."* (24:9)	**Yes** Mary Magdalene tells the disciples, *"I have seen the Lord."* (20:18)
After seeing the angels or men whom does Mary meet first?	Jesus (28:9)	Jesus (16:9)	The eleven apostles ((24:9)	Jesus (20:14)
Who does Jesus appear to first? Where and when did this take place?	The **2 Mary's**, on the **ways to Jerusalem after leaving the tomb** (28:9)	**Only Mary Magdalene** the location is **not indicated** but the timing has to be **after Mary fled the tomb** (16:8-9)	**Cleopas and another on the road to Emmaus 7 miles outside of Jerusalem** (24:13,18)	**Only Mary Magdalene at the tomb** (20:1, 11-14)
Is Mary permitted to touch Jesus after the resurrection?	Yes *"They came to him, **clasped his feet**..."* (28:9)	Not mentioned	Yes *"**Touch me** and see; a ghost does not have flesh and bones, as you see I have."* (24:39)	No Jesus says: *"**Do not hold on to me**, for I have not yet ascended to the Father. **Go instead to my brothers** and **tell them**, 'I am ascending to

my Father and your Father, to my God and your God." (20:17)

After examining the various "evidence", the witnesses (gospels) are found to contradict each other telling different versions of events without one thing in common among all their stories. Concerning the claims made about what happened to Jesus, the best that can be said is that the evidence presented by these witnesses (gospels) is inconclusive. One thing we can be certain of is that the witnesses are lying; it is impossible that they can all be telling the truth and all their versions could be accurate. I cannot believe one part of their entire story because they themselves cannot come to agreement on a single thing. They disagree on every single detail! The questions asked can only have one possible answer, but I have not gotten one straight answer to any part of their story at all. No part of their case can I turn to and say that "at least this part is true" because nothing they say has unanimous agreement. Based on the information supplied by these witnesses (gospels) it is unknown what happened to Jesus. Nothing these witnesses (gospels) have claimed can in good conscience be considered true and will not be admissible as testimony in Court. The case of Jesus is tabled until honest testimony can be presented, as it currently stands the ruling thus far is that there is no evidence to suggest that Jesus was crucified, died or that he was resurrected. This conclusion may be offensive to Christians because it means the core beliefs of Christianity are lies but this is how the bible says to determine whether testimony is true or false according to Mark 14:56-59 which ironically mentions people telling lies about Jesus :

"⁵⁶ **Many testified falsely** against him, but **their statements did not agree.** ⁵⁷ **Then some stood up and gave this false testimony** against him: ⁵⁸ "We heard him say, 'I will destroy this temple made with human hands and in three days will build another, not made with hands.'" ⁵⁹ Yet **even then their testimony did not agree**."

These verses from the English translation of the New International Version of the bible are so ironic that they are almost funny. Because in context the author is writing about people giving false testimony at the alleged trial of Jesus and he stipulates that the way to know it was false testimony was because "*their statements did not agree*". Thus according to Mark's biblical criteria of false testimony regarding Jesus the bible is also giving false testimony about Jesus as well. Then Mark mentions a specific lie that was told about Jesus where someone says Jesus said he would destroy the temple of Jerusalem and build another in 3 days. The bible says this was a lie that people falsely attributed to Jesus and that he never said such a thing. Yet the majority of Christians will tell you that Jesus said he would destroy the temple and rebuild it in 3 days and that he meant he would be crucified and raised and that the temple was also destroyed on the day he was crucified, therefore Christianity must be true. Yet historically in the real world the temple was not destroyed until 70 CE by the Romans following orders from Titus, and it hasn't been rebuilt. Biblically Mark says that people who lie about Jesus say that he said such a thing but he never did. However John's gospel says that Anas tried to hit a confession out of Jesus but couldn't since he didn't say anything wrong then or beforehand and since there were no testimonies given by anyone, either true or false, then Jesus was sent to Pontius Pilate. Whereas Luke says that the guards beat Jesus blindfolded telling him to prophesy and correctly say who hit him each time. At morning the priests and elders finally arrive and simply ask Jesus some questions and condemn him via his own words without any bearing testimony against him at all. While Matthew 26:49-56 say, "*The chief priests and the whole Sanhedrin were looking for false evidence against Jesus so that they could put him to death. 60 But they did not find any, though many false witnesses came forward. Finally two came forward 61 and declared, "This fellow said, 'I am able to destroy the temple of God and rebuild it in three days.'" 62 Then the high priest stood up and said to Jesus, "Are you not going to answer? What is this testimony that these men are bringing against you?" 63 But Jesus remained silent.*" Then Jesus gets condemned by his own words in a separate questioning period. Yet this gospel contradicts the gospels of Luke and John in that they mention Jesus openly challenging his enemies to bring anyone to testify against him saying that he said nothing secret and taught in public every day, to which no testimony is ever brought. While Mark says the testimony of those who claimed he said he would destroy the temple in 3 days and rebuild it in 3 days was false testimony because their testimony didn't agree. Yet Matthew cites this testimony which Mark says was false as being a truthful testimony and doesn't say anything about them disagreeing with each other at all. So Matthew says it's true and Mark says it's false and Luke 22 and John 18 both have 2 other different stories which say no testimonies were ever given by any aside from Jesus himself. Thus all we can do is accept Mark's criteria that the way to identify false testimony is that they don't agree. So according to the bible, not only are the gospels bearing false testimony about Jesus but the Christians bear false testimony about Jesus too. Forget Jesus for a moment, the bible doesn't even agree about the details of Judas! As the following charts of biblical contradictions regarding Judas prove:

Did Satan enter Judas before the Passover or after?

John 13:27	Luke 22:1-3
"Jesus answered, "It is the one to whom I will give this piece of bread when I have dipped it in the dish." Then, dipping the piece of bread, he gave it to **Judas, the son of Simon Iscariot**. ²⁷ **As soon as Judas took the bread, Satan entered into him.** So Jesus told him, "What you are about to do, do quickly." "	"Now the Festival of Unleavened Bread, called **the Passover, was approaching**, ² and the chief priests and the teachers of the law were looking for some way to get rid of Jesus, for they were afraid of the people. ³ **Then Satan entered Judas**, called Iscariot, one of the Twelve."

How did Judas die?

Matthew 27:5	Acts 1:18-19
"So **Judas threw the money into the temple and left. Then he went away and hanged himself.**"	"*(With the payment he received for his wickedness, Judas bought a field; there he fell headlong, his body burst open and all his intestines spilled out.* ¹⁹ Everyone in Jerusalem heard about this, so they called that field in their language Akeldama, that is, Field of Blood.)"

Did Judas keep the money or not?

Matthew 27:5-7	Acts 1:18
"So **Judas threw the money into the temple** and left. Then he went away and hanged himself. ⁶ **The chief priests picked up the coins and said, "It is against the law to put this into the treasury, since it is blood money." ⁷ So they decided to use the money to buy the potter's field** as a burial place for foreigners. "	"¹⁸ *(With the payment he received for his wickedness, **Judas bought a field**; there he fell headlong, his body burst open and all his intestines spilled out.*"

Likewise the bible contradicts itself regarding death details of the king Saul; who ruled before David.

How did Saul die?

1 Samuel 31:4-6	2 Samuel 1:6-10	2 Samuel 22:12	1 Chronicles 10:13-14
"*Saul said to his armor-bearer, "Draw your sword and run me through, or these uncircumcised fellows will come and run me through and abuse me." But his armor-bearer was terrified and would not do it; so **Saul took his own sword and fell on it**. When the armor-bearer saw that Saul was dead, he too fell on his sword and died with him.*"	""**I happened to be on Mount Gilboa**," the young man said, "and there was Saul, **leaning on his spear,** with the chariots and their drivers in hot pursuit. ⁷ When he turned around and saw me, he called out to me, and I said, 'What can I do?'" ⁸ "He asked me, 'Who are you?'"**An Amalekite,**' I answered. ⁹ "Then he said to me, 'Stand here by me and kill me! I'm in the throes of death, but I'm still alive.' ¹⁰ "So **I stood beside him and killed him**, because I knew that after he had fallen he could not survive. And I took the crown that was on his head and the band on his arm and have brought them here to my lord.""	" he went and took the bones of Saul and his son Jonathan from the citizens of Jabesh Gilead. (They had stolen their bodies from the public square at Beth Shan, where **the Philistines** had hung them after **they struck Saul down on Gilboa.**)"	"Saul died because he was unfaithful to the L<small>ORD</small>; he did not keep the word of the L<small>ORD</small> and even consulted a medium for guidance, ¹⁴ and did not inquire of the L<small>ORD</small>. So <u>**the L<small>ORD</small> put him to death**</u> and turned the kingdom over to David son of Jesse."

My question to Christians is that if I have to believe in the Easter Story for salvation, then what exactly is it that happened which I have to believe? Don't show me a movie about what I have to believe, show me what the Easter Story is according to the bible. People didn't use to have movies to watch, they had to use the bible to get the Easter Story. Although the bible was prohibited among the Christian populations and a crime to possess and read, only priests were allowed to read the bible so people would have had to learn what the bible said from their priest. At the outset during 382 CE soon after Roman Catholicism was declared the official religion of the Empire, Pope Damascus forbid those who weren't priests from reading the bible and priests were not allowed to teach the bible either. Bible translations were expressly prohibited and considered sinful. In 860 CE Pope Nicholas I banned the bible from being used in public by any who weren't Catholic priests. Another Pope Gregory renewed and supported the ban in 1073 CE. My former role model, Pope Innocent III in 1198 CE ruled that anyone caught reading a bible who wasn't a Catholic priest would be stoned to death by "soldiers of the Church". In 1229 CE it was prohibited for laymen to even possess the Old or New Testament. Eventually by the 14th century CE if you were found with a bible and were not a Catholic priest you would be whipped, have all your property confiscated and then would be burned to death at the stake. Now why would the Christian leaders go to such an extreme extent and mete out such punishment to those who possessed what they say is "*the word of God*"? Keep in mind being burned at the stake was for possession of the bible, one cannot even imagine what they would have done if a person was caught committing the crime of reading the bible. In fact the first man to translate the full bible into english was William Tyndale and because of committing such a "heretical blasphemous deed" he was burned to death in 1536 CE. This isn't ancient history either, because of a law passed by King Henry VIII it was illegal for women in England to read the bible until 1850 CE. Fortunately today we can read the bible ourselves and are no longer forced to rely on someone else telling us what it says or means. The bible is believed to have been written by eyewitnesses, but their stories crumble under **cross-examination**. If the bible is the word of God and Jesus is God then shouldn't there be a Gospel of Jesus in the bible? In fact shouldn't Jesus be the only author of the bible? If he were God he could've created the book easily within less than a second and mass produced it to the whole world so they could read the words of God. If Jesus is God and keeps appearing to people in visions saying what to do and telling people which bible is right then why doesn't he just write the right bible and send it down to us? I've read what the bible says Matthew, Mark, Luke and John say about Jesus and they use several quotations they say Jesus said. But why have 4 different versions of the same story if we have to believe it in order to avoid hell? The truth only has one edition, but there are many editions of the bible. They say that "*God works in mysterious ways*", but that's not mysterious that's just stupid. I'm confused and don't know which Easter Story to believe. If any Christian can tell me what the Easter Story is in chronological order of the events that allegedly took place using all the gospels and only the gospels for their information without any contradictions or omissions, then please tell me what the Easter Story I'm supposed to believe in is. I'm not going to watch a movie and simply believe what I see onscreen because I know the movie is fake and that nobody was filming Jesus 2000 years ago. The movie has false blood, false acting, false props, false sets, and a false plot. If that false plot is a religious belief then it would be a false religion.

Even if you watch the movies or read the gospels, the time it would have taken to enact the Last Supper, the agony in the Garden, the betrayal by Judas, the hauling before Caiaphas and the Sanhedrin, then before Pilate to the Hall of Judgment, then the visit to Herod Antipas mentioned only in Luke, and the return back to Pilate, Pilate's many different alleged speeches and washing of hands, then the scourging and arraying of Jesus in many different colored robes as a king in mockery, then the preparation of a Cross and the long painful journey to Golgotha, and finally the Crucifixion at Sunrise, these events are physically impossible to have all taken place within 12-15 hours as the movies and gospels state. Especially considering this allegedly took place on a major holiday night of Passover. It was an illegal sin in Jewish law for a Jewish tribunal of priests to sit at court at night, particularly the night of a religious feast. To do so would mean that no Jewish laws were respected and the Easter Story repeatedly depicts Jewish laws being violated and ignored, as well as inventing the rule about not killing on the Sabbath where the Old Testament says Jews repeatedly killed on the Sabbath cause God told them to. Likewise in Jewish courts prisoners were not asked questions and for trials involving capital offenses a minimum of 2 days were required for the trial to take place, it would have been sinful and illegal to do a trial in less time. For Jews to have crucified anyone at the sacred time of Passover they would have had to break at least 7 of their religious laws. Meaning they themselves would be punished according to their Jewish laws because of the sacrilegious manner they punished someone else. The Pharisees probably would've been crucified right alongside Jesus at the same time for breaking the Jewish laws. Except Jews didn't crucify people to kill them, they stoned them. It's implausible to believe Jews would arrange for Jesus to be killed for religious reasons on a religious holiday in a way that makes them violate their own religion. The illegality and confusion surrounding this alleged event is even in the bible verses of John 18:31-37

*"Pilate said, "Take him yourselves and judge him by your own law." "But **we have no right to execute anyone," they objected.** 32 This took place to fulfill what Jesus had said about the kind of death he was going to die. 33 Pilate then went back inside the palace, summoned Jesus and asked him, "Are you the king of the Jews?" 34 **"Is that your own idea," Jesus asked, "or did others talk to you about me?"** 35 "Am I a Jew?" Pilate replied. "Your own people and chief priests handed you over to me. What is it you have done?" 36 **Jesus said, "My kingdom is not of this world. If it were, my servants would fight to prevent my arrest by the Jewish leaders.** But now my kingdom is from another place." 37 "You are a king, then!" said Pilate. **Jesus answered, "You say that I am a king. In fact, the reason I was born and came into the world is to testify to the truth.** Everyone on the side of truth **listens to me**."*

The phrase "*My kingdom is not of this world.*" from this account in John is very famous, but nearly all who know of it have no idea what the context of it is. Interestingly only in John is this phrase ever spoken by

Jesus. According to Matthew, Mark and Luke, Jesus never said such a thing. Only John says Jesus said this. So that means either John had exclusive access to information which Mark, Luke and Matthew didn't, or God decided not to tell Matthew, Mark and Luke; or "John" made this stuff up. Regardless it is also interesting that John says Jesus said, "the reason I was born and came into the world is to testify to the truth." Because this means that even on the way to the cross, according to the bible Jesus is still saying his sole purpose in life is to "testify to the truth", not to be killed for the sins of mankind. Biblical Jesus also says that "Everyone on the side of truth listens to me." He doesn't say those on the side of truth worship me, or pray to me, or gain salvation through me, the bible says those on the side of truth <u>listen to Jesus</u>. Whereas if you tell Christians today that Jesus is said to have said to fast, to not be involved with interest/usury, to keep all 10 commandments and to worship the Creator only, most Christians will tell you "but Paul said" or "but John said" or "but the priest said". Most Christians simply don't care what Jesus said or even what the bible says Jesus said, instead they care what Christianity says. Whereas Muslims cannot be Muslim if they do not listen and obey Jesus. The thing is Muslims believe there is a difference between what the bible says Jesus said and what he actually said. Although most Christians think the bible is accurate when it puts words into Jesus' mouth. Thus according to these biblical words of Jesus in John, Christians are not "on the side of truth" since they don't listen to what they think Jesus said; listening in this context means obeying not just hearing. May God make us of those who hear and obey. Likewise when the bible says Jesus said <u>**_Is that your own idea," Jesus asked, "or did others talk to you about me?_**</u> this is a condemnation of getting beliefs/information about Jesus from indirect sources.

    Not only would the Jews be breaking the laws to execute Jesus, but Pontius Pilate and the Romans would've broken laws as well. To even have Jesus get in front of Pontius Pilate would have been illegal. Pontius Pilate was a busy man and had lots of court cases on a daily basis, just like modern man-made courts, cases had a waiting period before being brought before the judge. Jesus would not have been allowed to go to the head of the line and be judged until all the other court cases had been closed. The bible would have us believe that there were no other court cases in all of Judea and that Jesus was the first and only person in line to see the judge. Since it was a holiday, Pontius Pilate probably wouldn't even have been working that day and Jesus would have had to wait until a later court appointed date. Although let's say all protocol was ignored, that Pontius Pilate didn't take the day off and Jesus was the only one in line to see Pilate. To scourge or flog a man prior to conviction and sentencing would be illegal and cause Pilate to lose his job if he ordered it, as would the soldiers who did the illegal scourging/flogging. Then according to the Easter Story, Pontius Pilate gives the Jews a choice between freeing a convicted murderer named Barabbas or Jesus, to which they demand Pilate "Free Barabbas!" continuing to condemn Jesus despite him having already been allegedly fatally punished for nothing. If you watch the Easter movies the scourging that's depicted would have been equivalent to a death sentence. For the Jews to clamor for crucifixion would be like having someone put on trial facing the capital punishment while they are bleeding to death throughout the trial without receiving medical attention. No prosecutor would waste their time, energy and reputation in illegally pressing for the death sentence for an actively dying innocent man. The death of Jesus would have been an already foregone conclusion, so the Jews clamoring for crucifixion would have been breaking multiple religious and secular laws merely out of impatience. Never in the history of the world has there ever been such a trial seeking capital punishment for a man about to die. So when Pilate would have "washed his hands" he would have been washing the literal blood of Jesus off his hands that had dirtied them because of the fatal scourging he had ordered. This is equivalent to a judge shooting a man in court and then sentencing the man to the electric chair saying "*It's the chair that will kill him I'm completely innocent, this man's blood is on the prosecutor's hands*", while the condemned man begins to bleed to death all the way to the electric chair and the judge cleans the gun he shot him with. The character Barabbas is also a unique choice as the alternate option to be freed instead of Jesus. Barabbas was allegedly a political insurrectionist who committed murder of a political nature, he was a Jewish political assassin. Barabbas would be a convicted terrorist in the eyes of Pontius Pilate. It is inconceivable to believe that Rome would tolerate the freeing of a convicted political criminal at the behest of the very Jews whom they repressed and then execute an innocent person because the same Jews wanted it. In perspective this would be like the American military having Osama bin Laden in Guantanamo Bay and then letting him go free because Al-Qaeda asked them to execute the Pope and let Osama go free. That's basically what Catholics and Christians say happened with America being Rome, Osama being Barabbas and if Jesus were Pope. In reality Jews had practically zero influence on the pagan Roman government and if they clamored for Barabbas to be set free Rome would've killed him simply because of being too popular. The name Barabbas itself is another reason to doubt the authenticity of this historically impossible story, in Aramaic "Barabbas" literally means "son of the Father". But it gets even better when you read the English New International Version of the bible where Matthew 27:16-17 say,

"At that time they had <u>a well-known prisoner whose name was **Jesus Barabbas**</u>. So when the crowd had gathered, Pilate asked them, "Which one do you want me to release to you: <u>Jesus Barabbas, or Jesus</u> who is called the Messiah?""

In Aramaic the Jews saying to free Barabbas literally would have shouted "*Free the son of the Father!*" and if they said his full name as given in the gospel of Matthew they would have said "*Free Jesus the son of the Father!*" They don't base the movies off of these verses and they don't mention them in churches either. Allegedly every

Passover the Jews were allowed to choose one prisoner to be released each year; or so the story goes. In reality the Roman government did not allow Jews to have this special privilege, not during Passover or any other time of the year. Not only were Jews never granted this privilege, but no group within the Roman Empire was ever extended such a privilege for as long as the Roman Empire existed. Pontius Pilate would not have the authority to free a Roman prisoner, this would be another illegal action, especially if he gave Jews the choice of who was allegedly released and allowed them to select a Jewish enemy of the state. Considering that it was an unprecedented action never done by anyone in the Roman empire before or since and it involves a convicted political murderer, it's likely Pontius Pilate would have been executed for treason had he done what the Easter Story alleges. Considering the Roman government hated Jews, it is inconceivable to think this would happen. Yet the pagan Bablyonians did have this custom of releasing a prisoner at the annual Akitu festival and the ancient Greeks also had a similar rite. Historically Pontius Pilate remained in office long after these alleged events never suffering any recourse for the numerous illegal actions the bible says he had committed. The government definitely would've known if Pilate had done them if a new religion had sprung up and started sharing his exploits. "Washing his hands" of the matter also would have gotten him in trouble because Rome did not "give up power"; it took all the power it could and loved micro-management. For a governor to dismiss something and absolve Rome from having authority would have been another reason for immediate dismissal and punishment. In reality Pilate kept his post and was only replaced because of his repeated obstinate oppression and incitement of the Jews, that led them to rebel and riot. When Pontius Pilate first took office in 26 CE it was on the orders of the Roman emperor Tiberius. Right from the start Pilate antagonized the Jews, by placing standards with the graven image of the deified emperor all over the city of Jerusalem at night before his first day as governor. He knew this would piss off the Jews and that was his intention, to show them he was the boss and didn't care about their feelings. Pontius Pilate bullied the Jews again when he raided the sacred temple treasury and used the money to build aqueducts, when the Jews came to him and complained he had them beaten so severely some of them died. The real Pontius Pilate was the enemy of the Jews and hated by them. Pontius Pilate hated Jews as well, whereas the Easter Story's version of Pontius Pilate is basically a Jewish puppet. I say the Easter Story's Pilate because even the bible describes how Pilate hated Jews in Luke 13:1 " *Now there were some present at that time who told Jesus about the Galileans whose blood Pilate had mixed with their sacrifices.*" Meaning according to the bible Pilate mixed human Jewish blood with the sacred Jewish religious sacrifices. This would be comparable to mixing a prostitute's menstrual fluid with the wine at church. If Pilate was a puppet then the Romans surely wouldn't risk angering the Jews by putting a sign labeled "King of the Jews" above a crucified person they were killing on behalf of the Jews. The historical and biblical Pontius

Pilate is a completely different person than the Easter Story's Pontius Pilate. Therefore one must choose whether to believe in the Easter Story's Pontius Pilate, or the historical, or biblical one, because at the end of the day there was only one Pontius Pilate. Regardless of which is true, this means many are lying about who Pilate really was and what he did. Whichever version of Pontius Pilate is false, the fact is many have been deliberately duped.

      Did you know that there were private crucifixion contractors? Crucifixion in the Roman Empire was actually an industry that offered it's services to anyone who could afford them. Whenever a Roman wanted to punish or kill one of their slaves, they could legally just hire a contractor to build a wooden cross, hire a whip man to whip them and then crucify them to hang until they learned their lesson, or died from asphyxiation, dehydration or as a result of being scorched throughout the day and freezing at night. It was perfectly legal and a common practice for private citizens to crucify people they didn't like or for "fun". So the Roman government didn't have to play any part at all. All one needed to do to crucify someone was to sign the necessary business contracts with the laborers and make sure the person being crucified doesn't have powerful friends who would prevent it from happening or cause trouble. Yet if the Jews had stirred up such a mass frenzy as the bible says they did, then they could have easily gotten a private contractor to crucify Jesus legally. If they did do so then that may explain why the body would be taken down quickly because under no circumstances did the Roman state take down crucified persons early for any reason, in fact the whole point of a crucifixtion by the Roman state was so people could see the might of Rome and learn a lesson for days on end. Whereas to be extra moral/legal in case anyone tried to get Rome to stop the Jews from privately crucifying Jesus they could have said that since Jesus is a servant/slave of our God as he himself declared, then our God told us to do this and no Roman would disagree with it. This was because slaves had no legal rights and the Romans themselves had slaves serve in their pagan temples who could be legally crucified at the behest of the priests. The legal rights of the Roman Empire would shock many today, life was cheap, in the time of Jesus a husband could legally and even publicly kill his wife and never face any charges whatsoever. Whereas when the Roman state itself wanted to kill someone they just did it, they didn't have long trials or appeals as the bible depicts. So the biblical death of Jesus can be realistic if the Jews crucified Jesus all by themselves. But why would anyone try to say the Jews manipulated the Roman government to kill a prophet if they didn't and the Roman government had no part to play? Wouldn't involving the Roman government make the Jews seem better? Actually no. Until very recently with the creation of the state of Israel, Christian civilization has repeatedly refused to be publicly ruled by Jews or allow them political rights. This is because of the bible stories of the Jews playing the Roman government like a puppet in order to illegally murder a prophet. This biblical depiction of Jews has also caused many to think Jews have been sinisterly controlling and manipulating the world governments for centuries. Now I'm no friend of anyone who believes in Judaism, whereas Jewishness itself is just an ethnicity and incidentally I have Muslim friends who are Jewish. Yet despite my enmity for Judaism I know 100% that Jews are not running the world behind the scenes. While Jews are guilty for many evil things, we can't go to extremes. Yes some shady stuff does go down and some Jews play a role, but the notion of a mass conspiracy gives them too much undeserved credit. It is because of such paranoid doctrines that genocide occurs. Satan is the one who is really behind the global conspiracy, but the big secret is that all his influential puppets are in satanic cahoots unintentionally. It's because they all have the same fundamental goals that they seem to be working together, but in reality they don't intend to.

    Had Jesus really been crucified then where was the resistance from his followers? When combined the gospels can seem to say Peter cut off the ear of a soldier, which Jesus heals the wounded arrestor and tells Peter that God could save him if he wanted by sending angels. That combo-story may explain why the disciples didn't attempt a rescue, but surely they would have at least demonstrated against the illegal actions being taken by the Jews and Romans. They are not even mentioned as having shouted out for mercy, or offered words of comfort to Jesus. The movies would have us believe that his companions just stood by and watched silently, with Christians assuming they were taking notes for future generations. If they were there to witness it then they would have vocally protested or comforted Jesus. If they were silent lest they have the mob turn on them, then they would have been in hiding too afraid to risk getting caught and exposed for being associates. The bible also has a story about Peter apparently "denying Christ" 3 times before a rooster crows in the morning on Friday. Although "denying Christ" in a biblical context means disassociating oneself and not following him, it has nothing to do with denying divinity, or trinity, or him being a son of God; biblically it meant not following the ideas of Jesus or his teachings. Peter had been identified as learning from Jesus and suspected of holding the same beliefs and ideas. Jesus allegedly told Peter he would deny him 3 times before the rooster crowed **once** according to John 13:38, or 3 times before the rooster crowed **twice** according to Mark 14:30 and 14:72, and this is just hours after the famous "Last Supper" where Peter adamantly said he would never deny Jesus. To reconcile the discrepancy some will say that Peter denied Jesus 6 times total, 3 before the rooster crowed once and then 3 before it crowed twice. Yet the bible only mentions 3 times total in each gospel. Mark and John have 2 different prophecies, Mark says his was fulfilled but John doesn't say his was, but they were both two different prophecies regardless. Christians just combine them both together and say both came true, because the priest and movies say so. However the movies/plays/stories mention John's prophecy, then use Mark's data to say it was fulfilled, then use John's rooster only crowing once, then finish if off with Mark's Peter saying Jesus' prophecy in Mark was certainly true except they say Mark's peter said John's rooster crowing once prophecy was true and change the words in the scripts. Then Christians ask me why don't I believe the story, and I say because I read the bible whereas they just heard a story and got told it's from the bible when it isn't. This same Peter is believed to have been such a devout companion that he slices off the ear of a guard who allegedly arrested Jesus, as told only in the gospel of John, but then he has such a rapid change of heart that he is afraid of some petty servants when they accuse him of having known Jesus. This Peter wasn't afraid to spill blood for Jesus, but hours later is so scared that he denies even knowing the name of Jesus? Yet this unstable character is supposed to be "the rock" upon which Jesus built his Church? How can someone go from physically fighting the police who came to arrest their friend, wounding and disfiguring them, only stopping when their friend/prophet/God(if you believe some Christians) tells them to, to being a complete coward denying even knowing their friend's/prophet's/God's(if you believe some Christians) name hours later? If Peter really did deny Jesus so quickly with such little pressure applied and he was the #1 companion of Jesus and leader of the church after Jesus departed then it's no wonder the religion Jesus taught got corrupted so soon to such a great extent. The common companions of Muhammad had much greater loyalty to him under greater persecution/pressure than Peter biblically had to Jesus in his alleged hour of need. Even when Pharaoh tried to kill Moses there was a believer who spoke in defense of Moses to deter the execution. The same applies to other companions of other prophets, biblically Jesus though he is claimed to be the ultimate prophet who is semi-divine has some of the least loyal followers ever portrayed by the bible, and it's because of that many slanders are made against the other prophets to balance the negatives to make Jesus still seem extremely superior to other prophets when in reality Jesus simply had more loyal followers than the bible portrays. The problem is the bible doesn't really portray the best followers of Jesus but portrays accounts of those who later Christians thought/decreed were the best from their perspective though they had no genuine proof from Jesus for their claims. Thus you have characters like Paul and Luke who never even met Jesus according to the bible itself being considered top figures in Christianity despite their acknowledged distance and lack of relationship to/with the real Jesus. Even if Jesus had healed the wounded man's ear(which only Luke says was healed, and only John says Peter was the one who cut it off), the guards would have still arrested or killed Peter for assaulting an officer and inhibiting an arrest. If Peter were to become a coward at anytime it would have been at the time of arrest. If Peter stayed firm when the arrest took place then it is unreasonable to believe he would crumble when people asked him if he knew Jesus. Although today many believe this allegedly apostating persona is a "rock" and the solid foundation which the papal hierarchy was built upon. A rock doesn't have cracks, a cracked rock becomes rocks disunited and divided. If Peter did crack and deny affiliation with Jesus or belief in his doctrine, he would not have been the "solid foundation" for which to build a religious institution from. Everyone else is depicted as having remained firm in their faith silently to Jesus devoutly, despite everyone fleeing at the time of arrest, (one even fleeing naked) but the 2nd in command leader of the group apparently was the only one who cracked and denied knowing Jesus despite John saying he only got into the courtyard because another disciple known to the high priest(probably as a disciple of Jesus, maybe even Judas himself or else Judas would've informed him) got permission for Peter to enter. All this makes Peter the least qualified person to be leader of the Church and it is unlikely he would have had any credibility among the companions had this denial taken place regardless of whether Jesus predicted it or not. Historically Peter wasn't considered to be the first Pope or bishop of Rome until the 4th century, after Roman Catholicism was the dominant form of Christianity. The bible story also neglects to mention all the people whom Jesus healed and taught, where were they during the trial and crucifixion? How could it be that not one of the students or miracle cases of Jesus testified on his behalf vocally or physically protesting his crucifixion? This was their religion teacher and leader being illegally murdered at the holiest time of the year by pagans. This just wouldn't fly, a revolt if not a revolution would have ensued had Jesus truly been crucified or killed. Coincidentally Mark 14:1-2 says the very same: "*Now the Passover and the Festival of Unleavened Bread were only two days away, and the chief priests and the teachers of the law were scheming to arrest Jesus secretly and kill him.* 2 "**But not during the festival," they said, "or the people may riot."** (then the bible says they did it during that very time people would've rioted had it actually been done.)

     I also say crucified or killed because crucifixtion doesn't mean death and not everyone who believes Jesus died thinks he was crucified. For instance in 1928 CE Joseph Rutherford as president of the Jehovah's Witnesses said members should discard crosses as unnecessary jewelry. Then in 1931 CE Rutherford began to teach Jesus wasn't crucified but staked instead. Prior to this Jehovah's Witnesses believed and taught that Jesus was crucified and would display crosses on their material, with their alleged founder Charles Taze Russell even having a cross on his pyramid tombstone. Rutherford made this doctrinal change because he knew pagans believed in crucified saviors so he thought it couldn't have happened to Jesus since he thought his Christian religion was true and not based on pagan beliefs. So instead of rejecting the false pagan doctrine of a murdered son of God savior he just changed the props so they were less pagan and made his stake story. Since an excuse had to be made to justify dropping the pagan Cross but keeping the pagan son of God death he said the Greek word used at that time for cross doesn't really mean cross because originally it meant stake instead of cross. The funny thing is that pagan religions also had various myths where their son of God savior was staked as well, so they dropped one pagan prop because of it's pagan significance only to adopt another pagan prop. Now I could refute this unbiblical belief but the Christians already have, I just mention this to show that Christians themselves can't even agree on a story and refute each other's stories. Whereas those who do believe in the cross then have multiple different types of crosses they say it was. There is the crux simplex (I shape), crux decussata (X shape), crux commissa (T shape), crux immissa (t shape), furca (A shape), patibulum(Π) shape. Then they dispute on whether he was nailed or tied to the cross. Then they dispute whether he was nailed with 2 nails, one for both hands above the head and one for both feet, or 3 nails one for each hand and one for both feet, or 4 nails one for each apendage. Whereas also if he was nailed in each arm then was it in the palms or in the wrists? Nobody has any solid proof to back up any of the various answers to any of these questions, it's all conjecture.

    Another detail concerning the Easter story is that there were Roman guards stationed at the alleged tomb of Jesus. The reason it isn't in the previously included chart is because Matthew is the only gospel which mentions this occurrence, Mark, Luke and John make absolutely no reference to it. The movies typically portray 2 Roman soldiers at the tomb. Now why in the world would the Roman Empire post highly trained highly paid troops at the tomb of a dead enemy of the state for numerous days? As foolish as this sounds already, if roman soldiers were posted it would constitute them breaking the sabbath by working on it, whereas they allegedly took Jesus down from the cross purposely to avoid breaking the very same sabbath. This would be an expensive contradiction of government policy because the roman soldiers would've been paid. Since they would need guards around the clock to stay awake there would have to be numerous shifts and they all would've been getting paid overtime. Christians who accept this story say there were 4 guards stationed in shifts of 4 hours each. Which means approximately 24 Roman soldiers were assigned this job of standing by a tomb for an enemy of the state. Realistically this could have potentially cost the Roman government the equivalent of hundreds of thousands of dollars. Since the Roman military kept records of every payment they made, in order to justify their large budget, this expensive operation would've been recorded and reported to the Emperor. No such record of any operation exists among the Roman records from that time period and surely it would have been a scandalous report had it ever been discovered by the government or the citizenry. However if no report was made out of embarrassment, then the government officials in charge of this posting would have been asked about the missing funds and where they went and why. So numerous people would've lost their jobs, at the least, had any soldiers been posted at a crucified man's tomb. But not only does the bible say soldiers were stationed there but it says that the body of the guy they were guarding escaped. Which makes this tale even more scandalous for the Roman government.

Imagine paying about 24 highly trained soldiers to guard an apparently dead body and then it disappears. Legally if Roman soldiers let a live prisoner escape they would be executed, so imagine what punishment would be given to those who allowed dead prisoners to escape! This would have been history's largest example of government incompetence that would have become famous across the world for ages among Christians and non-Christians alike. If any of the alleged resurrection versions were true then it would mean these Roman soldiers would've been the first to have known and one would expect they would've become Christians. However nobody in all of Christendom says any of these Roman soldiers believed, in fact the soldiers are never mentioned again. Surely both the Christians and the Romans would have wanted the testimony of the Roman soldiers. Yet no historical records exist of any such testimony as to what the alleged Roman soldiers said about the disputed events, there are no records of testimony from either Christians or non-Christians. Thus we can only conclude that there were no Roman soldiers posted at the alleged tomb of Jesus, despite what the movies and the gospel of Matthew say. If there were soldiers there then whoever went to visit the tomb would have been pretty stupid to visit knowing that soldiers who considered Jesus a bad guy were guarding it. Another remarkable event alleged to have occurred after the alleged resurrection of Jesus is also exclusively mentioned in Matthew. The gospels of Mark, Luke and John never mention this detail, it is only found in Matthew. The English translation of the New International Version of the bible verses of Matthew 27:51-55 state:

> "[51] *At that moment the curtain of the temple was torn in two from top to bottom. The earth shook, the rocks split* [52] *and the tombs broke open.* **The bodies of many holy people who had died were raised to life.** [53] **They came out of the tombs after Jesus' resurrection and went into the holy city and appeared to many people.** [54] *When the centurion and those with him who were guarding Jesus saw the earthquake and all that had happened, they were terrified, and exclaimed, "Surely he was the Son of God!"* [55] *Many women were there, watching from a distance.* **They had followed Jesus from Galilee to care for his needs**.*"*

The gospel of Matthew says that not only did Jesus rise from the dead, but many people who had died were raised to life. Not only were these people raised from the dead, but they went into Jerusalem and were seen by many people with the bible specifically mentioning witnesses to this event including roman guards and women who came to care for Jesus' "needs". But what needs could a resurrected son of God or God incarnate have? Matthew fails to mention one name of a saint that was raised, as well as neglecting to say how long they stayed on earth after being raised and what happened to them. In fact they are never mentioned again as if they weren't even important or significant to his story. Such a spectacle seems like it wouldn't have escaped the attention of anyone. Allegedly a graveyard had the dead people come out of the grave into the city; it was basically a zombie invasion as people would say today. Despite Matthew saying women and roman guards and the people of Jerusalem witnessed this, not one historian or any source has ever mentioned this supernatural phenomenon. Not even Christians mention this event, it is only in the gospel of Matthew. Likewise with the alleged earthquake, many philosophers and scientists at that time including Seneca and Pliny the Elder painstakingly recorded all earthquakes that took place, yet there is no record of such an earthquake taking place in Jerusalem during the time period stated in the gospel of Matthew. Surely the anti-Christians wouldn't have hidden an earthquake just because it had Christian significance? This line of thinking means that for the bible to be true, every historian, philosopher and scientist during the time of Jesus were all liars who never told the truth about anything. This is quite an extreme statement to make, especially when as we've seen the gospels themselves fail to agree, with that logic the very gospels of the bible are false because they fail to mention everything the other gospels say, including Matthew's earthquake. If it weren't for the gospel of Matthew no one would have ever thought such an earthquake or the mass resurrection of a graveyard took place at all. Certainly if this actually happened then someone other than Matthew would have recorded it as well. Even if one takes the position that non-Christians purposely would've neglected to tell about the day the dead people entered Jerusalem, which is hard to believe it would be kept a secret, this doesn't explain why Mark, Luke, John, Paul and every other Christian writer neglects to mention this. It is interesting to note that none of the Easter Story movies or plays include this event despite it being part of the bible and what the gospel of Matthew says took place. It's understandable for a producer to leave it out if they think Matthew's fable to be false, but it is dishonest for these Easter portrayals to include an earthquake destroying the temple and the guard saying *"Surely he was the Son of God!"* without mentioning the masses of dead people who rose and entered Jerusalem. The resurrected corpses are mentioned in between the earthquake and the centurion's statement. This picking and choosing done by the producer to tell a story that is marketable is dishonest, but the producers are not religious teachers so it is understandable. Unfortunately not only is this picking and choosing of the biblical Easter Story done by movie producers it is also done by priests and preachers. Think of all the times you have heard of the alleged resurrection of Jesus being told to you in church, or by some evangelical Christian, how many times have you also heard that graveyards full of holy people were resurrected along with Jesus and entered the city of Jerusalem? Yet this is what the gospel of Matthew says happened. To me a graveyard of people coming back to life entering a major city of living people is the most exciting part. Why would they leave that out? It is highly unlikely any Christian preacher would ever dare to tell people what the gospel of Matthew says in 27:52. They will use verses 51 and 54 when talking about Easter, but this is taking the bible out of context. <u>Taking text out of context leaves you with nothing but a "con".</u> For instance all the Christians love to say how the centurion said "*Surely he was the Son of God!*" and the movies and plays usually always make it a climatic scene, but there's a problem in that this statement is just one version. The biblical version in Luke 23:47 says: "*The centurion, seeing what had happened, praised God and said, "Surely this was a <u>righteous man</u>.*" Obviously there is a huge difference between saying someone was "*the Son of God*" vs. saying they were "*a righteous man*" yet both versions can't be true. Depending on which verse one chooses they will have completely different religious beliefs. But at the end of the day this centurion, if he existed, is not qualified to determine for the world who/what Jesus was. Really who cares what a centurion said? Nevertheless while I understand Christian preachers and producers must pick and choose in order to tell a story, the problem is they deceitfully tell a story without telling Christians that they pick and choose different parts of the bible completely ignoring and rejecting all the other parts of the bible which contradict the story which they manufactured. If you read the bible horizontally, or each gospel with retention of what you've read, you will discover the infamous Easter Story is not found directly in the bible at all. It is a conflation of many different gospels with some information from Matthew, some from Mark, some from John, some from Luke and some from Hollywood. Realistically the story of Jesus' alleged crucifixion, death and resurrection is taken out of context and disagrees with all the gospels of Matthew, Mark, Luke and John and even Paul. If the authors of these gospels or Paul were to hear the Easter Story today they would all say that it disagrees with what they wrote, preached and believed in. To say the Easter story is based on what the bible says would be akin to me saying this book is based on what the dictionary says. Just because the words are found in the book does not mean they are the basis for the derivative work. Picking and choosing a couple of phrases from one gospel and combining them with other phrases from other gospels in order to create a flowing narrative is dishonest and a misrepresentation. The Easter Story has neither a historical basis nor a biblical basis. The Easter Story is deceptive, the truth is not deceptive, Satan is deceptive, God is not deceptive. Therefore the Easter Story seems to be inspired by Satan and not God. Even if one believes the bible to be the word of God, because the Easter Story is not based on the bible the Easter Story is still not inspired by God. Aside from cultural traditions, theatre and unsubstantiated conjecture there are no other sources which support the narrative of the Easter Story. The problem is that all the different Christian versions of what happened to Jesus are invalid and false historically, scientifically, biblically, politically and religiously.

    So where did the Easter story come from originally? To know that we must know the character Paul. Paul was originally known as Saul. Saul was a Pharisee of a certain Jewish sect that both John and Jesus referred to as vipers advising believers to stay far away from them (including Saul). Saul was actually killing the people who followed Jesus, systematically eliminating every Christian community he came across, one by one. A little know fact about Saul was that he had proposed to a woman with amber hair named Poppaea Sabina asking her to marry him, she turned him down went to Rome and ended up marrying the Roman emperor Nero. It's not every day someone's pagan girlfriend says no to marriage and then runs off to marry the most powerful, famous and wealthy man on the planet. Saul must have been bitterly devastated and in desperate need for emotional validation, who wouldn't be in that situation? On the way to Damascus to kill more Christians, Saul allegedly had a vision which blinded him and was told he was called to a special mission by Jesus. There are different contradicting biblical versions of this vision, some say he was alone, another says a certain number of people were with him with other contradictions over the number of people that were with him (if any) and whether they also heard what Saul was told or not. Then there is a great deal of controversy over what the vision actually was, whether it was Jesus, or if it was light, or what, but whatever happened on the road to Damascus Saul/Paul decided to change his approach to Christianity. Saul went into Damascus proclaiming that he converted to Christianity. In Damascus the Christians there said he was a liar, saying that he was planning to kill them before and now he was trying to corrupt their religion by following the strategy of joining them because he couldn't beat them in an attempt to distort and destroy Christianity from the inside. Saul/Paul was chased out of town, forced to leave the city at night in a basket-case, most likely as an emotional and spiritual basketcase as well. The biblical book of Acts says the Jews caused him to leave but this is spurious, because the whole reason Saul was going to Damascus was to kill Christians because no Jews were there who could kill them. Thus for Acts to then say that Jews caused the Christian Saul to leave contradicts the very reason Jewish Saul was going there. If Jews were there Saul wouldn't have went, if Saul went then it means if there were Jews in Damascus they couldn't harm anybody, especially not a killing machine like Saul. After Damascus, according to his biblical letter to the Galatians, Saul/Paul spent 3 years in Arabia with no record of what he was doing. Perhaps he went there searching for someone as part of his bounty hunter job, or maybe went to visit the Jews of Madinah who taught that the Torah said a prophet would be coming to that city. Next Saul/Paul resurfaced in Jerusalem and began teaching his theology to the actual companions of Jesus such as Peter, Barnabas, James and Thomas. The companions of Jesus rebuked Saul/Paul saying he was spreading heresy. Peter, considered to be the leading companion and "rock of the Church", wanted to kill Saul/Paul. Before they were able to kill Saul, who changed his name to Paul so as not to be associated with his past slaughtering of Christians, Barnabas (the 2nd closest companion of Jesus) convinced Peter and the others to spare Saul/Paul and teach him the truth about Jesus. Barnabas was the only companion of Jesus who thought Saul/Paul was sincere, but just confused. Up until this time the followers of Jesus only preached to Jews as per the instructions of Jesus:

Matthew 10:5-6 "*⁵ These twelve Jesus sent out with the following instructions: "Do not go among the Gentiles or enter any town of the Samaritans. ⁶ Go rather to the lost sheep of Israel."*"

Matthew 15:22-26 "*²² A Canaanite woman from that vicinity came to him, crying out, "Lord, Son of David, have mercy on me! My daughter is demon-possessed and suffering terribly." ²³ Jesus did not answer a word. So his disciples came to him and urged him, "Send her away, for she keeps crying out after us." ²⁴ **He answered**, "I was sent only to the lost sheep of Israel."²⁵ The woman came and knelt before him. "Lord, help me!" she said. ²⁶ He replied, "It is not right to take the children's bread and toss it to the dogs.""*

    Saul/Paul accompanied Barnabas in his journeys. However Barnabas still strictly limited his teaching to Jews because the Pagans weren't fit to understand the message of Jesus, as evidenced by the account in the English translation of the New International Version of the Bible where the pagans mistakenly think Paul and Barnabas are gods and want to worship them in Acts 14:11-13,"*¹¹ When the crowd saw what Paul had done, they shouted in the Lycaonian language, **"The gods have come down to us in human form!"** ¹² **Barnabas they called Zeus, and Paul they called Hermes** because he was the chief speaker. ¹³ The priest of Zeus, whose temple was just outside the city, brought bulls and wreaths to the city gates because he and the crowd wanted to offer sacrifices to them.*" Paul eventually built up a name for himself using the credibility of the disciple Barnabas. In old age Barnabas retired to what is modern day Cyprus giving up on correcting Paul's heretical views, primarily because Paul refused to travel with John Mark who was Barnabas' Greek translator. Paul basically made Barnabas choose between using Paul as a translator or not traveling with Paul at all. Barnabas chose to retire rather than trust Paul to translate for him correctly. Paul then went out on his own to preach, using the contacts and credentials he obtained when traveling with the disciple Barnabas. Paul had never met Jesus during his time on earth. Luke acted as Paul's physician and likewise had never actually met or heard Jesus during his time on earth. Mark was the scribe of Peter and also never actually saw or heard Jesus while he was on earth. When Paul first began preaching, no Jews or Christians would listen to him and maintained he was a heretic of both religions. After having no success, he began preaching his Pauline version of Christianity to pagans who hadn't heard the teachings of Jesus before and were also unfamiliar with the teachings of Judaism. In the English translation of the New International Version of the bible Romans 15:20 Paul cites his reasons why: "²⁰ **It has always been my ambition** to preach the gospel where Christ was not known, so that I would not be building on someone else's foundation." It is rather suspicious that a "follower of Jesus" would not want to build on his foundation but would want to preach to people who didn't know Christ. This implies that Paul did not see Jesus in a vision nor change his religion, because if that were the case he would be obligated to teach those who heard of Christ the new updates he had learned from Jesus, but as he unequivocally states he "always" wanted to preach "*where Christ was not known*". That Paul says "*it has always been my ambition*" is clearly a lie. It certainly was not Paul's ambition to preach the message of Jesus when he was killing Christians under the name of Saul. So what does Paul mean when he says, "*It has always been my ambition to preach the gospel where Christ was not known*"? Did Paul always intend to preach a religion to gentiles? What "gospel" is Paul referring to since the biblical gospels weren't written at that time? Was it just a slip of the tongue? But this sentence is in the bible, surely the bible doesn't contain any "slips of the tongue" or errors, does it? Paul's brand of Christianity was distinctly different from the others. Paul later claimed that God personally revealed to him (technically this means he claims to be a prophet) that no Jewish laws had to be observed and that Jesus had replaced it all with a "new covenant", abrogating everything that came before him including the 10 commandments. When Paul told this to Jews and Christians he was laughed out of town, because they knew Jesus was circumcised, kept Kosher and stressed keeping all of the Law given to Moses in spirit and practice to the letter. As Matthew 5:17-18 says Jesus said " *Do not think that I have come to abolish the Law or the Prophets; I have not come to abolish them but to fulfill them. 18 For truly I tell you, until heaven and earth disappear, not the smallest letter, not the least stroke of a pen, will by any means disappear from the Law* " The real flesh and blood Jesus publicly accused the Rabbi's of ignoring the major principles and focusing too much on the minute specifics while breaking the Law of Moses themselves. Jesus never said the laws weren't to be followed, or anything about a "new covenant" rather he exposed the hypocrisy of the Jewish leaders who didn't follow the laws of Moses as they were supposed to be followed and corrupted the laws to suit their desires, following that which they pleased and/or ignoring the stuff they didn't like. The problem according to Jesus was not with the law at all, the problem was with the way people weren't following the law. May God protect us from falling into hypocrisy like the Pharisees. Paul said the unrealistic law of God was the problem and that God himself knew the law was too hard to follow. So therefore the body/blood of Jesus allegedly liberated everyone from having to follow any of God's laws. However Jesus was not on earth to comment on Paul's claims. Strangely those who personally met Jesus in the flesh all said that Paul was lying about the prophet Jesus. Those whom Paul was formerly persecuting rejected him and his new interpretation of the person of Jesus. Without success preaching to Jews or Christians, Paul went to pagan gentiles. With the pagans Paul had tons of success in spreading his religious views, with his followers calling themselves Christians even though they were technically Paulians. Like Paul they never actually met Jesus while he was on earth. Yet Christians are never told or taught what these pagans who didn't know about Christ already believed before they were exposed to Paul's teachings. However it is crucially important to know what these pagans believed about God and religion. We must learn what their pagan rituals were so we can be aware of the circumstances and settings Paul was walking into. Thereby we can appreciate the difficulty he would encounter in having his teachings accepted by people who had never heard of Jesus.

In Ancient times the Ankh cross ☥ was adored in Egypt thousands of years before Jesus was born. Not by Jews or Christians, but by pagans. The Catholic Church officially adopted the cross symbol approximately 600 years after Jesus was believed to have been crucified. The early Christians of North Africa even rejected the pagan wooden cross after Tertullian condemned it. One of the famous fathers of the Church Tertullian conceded that the <u>pagans worshiped crucified saviors</u> who would be hanging on a cross. Tertullian considered it blasphemy for Christians to have anything to do with crosses because they were a pagan symbol frequently glorified in rituals of idolatry, *"Crosses, moreover, we Christians neither venerate nor wish for. You indeed who consecrate gods of wood venerate wooden crosses, perhaps as parts of your gods. For your very standards, as well as your banners, and flags of your camps, what are they but crosses gilded and adorned? Your victorious trophies not only imitate the appearance of a simple cross, but also that of a man affixed to it."* The bishop Tertullian believed Jesus was crucified, yet still rejected the cross as a pagan object and un-Christian. Despite being a Christian, Tertullian said Christianity borrowed the cross and atonement concept of *"dying for the sins of mankind"* from pagans.

The original form of the first cross was the initial letter T of the pagan Babylonian god Tammuz, written like "†". During Babylonian baptism ceremonies, the pagan priests of Tammuz would make the sign of the cross on the forehead of the baptized. When praying the worshippers of Tammuz would make the sign of the "†" over their heart. The Babylonian virgins would also wear this symbol of Tammuz around their necks as a sign of their faith. During March and April for 40 days the pagans would mourn the death of Tammuz who was thought to be the only begotten son of the sun-god and moon goddess. The bible refers specifically to this 40-day period of mourning for the pagan god Tammuz, when it took place in Jerusalem with the pagan idol Tammuz in the temple during the Babylonian occupation.

Ezekiel 8:14-20 "*14 Then he brought me to the entrance of the north gate of the house of the Lord, and <u>I saw women sitting there, mourning the god Tammuz.</u> 15 <u>He said to me, "Do you see this, **son of man**? You will see things that are even more detestable than this."</u> 16 He then brought me into the inner court of the house of the Lord, and there at the entrance to the temple, between the portico and the altar, were about twenty-five men. With their backs toward the temple*

of the Lord and their faces toward the east, <u>they were bowing down to the sun</u> in the east. ¹⁷ *He said to me, "Have you seen this, son of man? <u>Is it a trivial matter for the people of Judah to do the detestable things they are doing here</u>? Must they also fill the land with violence and continually arouse my anger?* **Look at them putting the branch to their nose!**
¹⁸ *Therefore I will deal with them in anger; I will not look on them with pity or spare them. Although they shout in my ears, I will not listen to them."*

Ezekiel says, "*I saw women sitting there, mourning the god Tammuz*" this indicates that he didn't hear what they were saying but was able to visibly identify them. Most probably because they were wearing the cross of Tammuz around their neck. The verses also repeatedly stress how Ezekiel saw, seen and will see; indicating that the witnessing of detestable things was entirely visual. That verse 15 refers to Ezekiel as "son of man" is also important because many Christians think "son of man" means "son of God" whenever Jesus is referred to by such a title but clearly Ezekiel was not a son of God; thus we can deduce that the phrase "son of man" does not mean "son of God". It continues to explain how the people were bowing (in some translations worshipping) the Sun. God didn't think it was trivial and when they "put the branch to their nose" it caused God to cut ties with them so that he wouldn't answer their prayers because of them worshipping falsehood. But what does it mean that they "put the branch to their nose"? It's simple really, whenever believers worshiped they put their nose on the ground in prostration to pray, thus "*putting the branch to their nose*" means they worshiped the branch. Since Tammuz and Sun worship is also mentioned, in context it literally means these people worshiped the cross. In actual meaning they worshiped the idea that the Sun or Son of the Sun God "Tammuz" died for the forgiveness of their sins. As a result the bible tells us that God said: "*Therefore I will deal with them in anger; I will not look on them with pity or spare them. Although they shout in my ears, I will not listen to them."*

Some pagans believed that the "sun of God" was their savior instead of a son of God. They thought the sun was visibly hung on a cross or "crossified" when it passed through the equinoxes. People in northern climates were "*saved*" by the "crossification" of the sun when it crossed over the equatorial line into the season of spring, at the vernal equinox. Coincidentally Easter is always the first Sunday after the full moon of vernal equinox. The sun gave out a saving heat and light to the world stimulating the generative organs of animal and vegetable life. They believed the sun was the light of the world for which all life on earth was eternally dependent upon. The 12 months of the year were religiously significant as well as the 12 signs of the zodiac which are seated in 4 groups of 3 in representation of the 4 seasons. The pagan sun worshippers of solar cults believed the following about the "*sun of God*":

- The Sun of God was the "*light of the world*"
- The Sun of God dies for three days at the winter solstice, to be born again on December 25th.
- The Sun of God is "*born of a virgin*" referring to the "virgin" moon and the constellation of Virgo.
- The Sun of God has his "birth" attended by the "*bright Star*" Sirius and by "*Three Kings*" representing the 3 stars in the belt of Orion.
- The Sun of God at its zenith, or 12 noon, is in the house of the heavenly temple of the "Most High"; thus "he" begins his "Father's work" at "age" 12.
- The Sun of God enters into each sign of the zodiac at 30 degrees, thus begins his ministry at "age" 30.
- The Sun of God is "*anointed*" when its rays dip into the sea.
- The Sun of God "*calms the sea*" and "*walks on water*" referring to its reflection.
- The Sun of God is the "Lion" in Leo, the hottest time of the year.
- The Sun of God triumphantly "rides an ass and her foal" into the "City of Peace" when it enters the sign of Cancer.
- The Sun of God is "betrayed" by the constellation of the Scorpion, which is the time of year when the sun loses strength.
- The Sun of God was "*crucified*" or "*crossified*" and "*hung on a cross*" when it passed through equinoxes with the "*crucifixion of the sun of God*" saving the northern people when it crossed the equatorial line in the spring at the vernal equinox known as Easter.
- The Sun of God is "crucified" between the two thieves of Sagittarius and Capricorn.
- The Sun of God would darken on the day it dies.
- The Sun of God wears a corona, or "*crown of thorns*" or halo.
- The Sun of God would seem to be motionless as if it were dead for nearly 3 days during the vernal equinox before "*rising from the dead on the third day*".

- The Sun of God was the Word or Logos of God
- The Sun of God "*cometh on clouds, and every eye shall see him*"
- The Sun of God rising makes it the "*savior of mankind*" since the cold darkness of night leaves.
- The Sun of God returns to judge the living and the dead on a "white horse" or cloud.
- The Sun of God ultimately defeats the "*Prince of Darkness*" or the nighttime darkness.

In Rome the mythical founder Romulus was allegedly born of a virgin priestess of Vesta who had sworn herself to celibacy before claiming to be impregnated by the divine. The king didn't believe it and tossed Romulus and his twin Remus into the river to die. Romulus is believed to have been saved by a heavenly wind and proclaimed to be the "son of god". After "post-death" appearances he became known as Quirinus who is a part of the Archaic Trinity which was worshiped by the Romans. The sun was also thought to have grown dark on the day of the death of Romulus.

In Greece Dionysus was believed to have been born in a manger on December 25th. Allegedly crucified after a final supper with his 12 companions, he told his enemies "*You know not what you are doing.*" Dionysius was thought to have risen from the dead on March 25th. He was also symbolically eaten in a Eucharistic ceremony as a means of purification. He was called "*King of Kings*", "*God of Gods*", "*Redeemer*", "*Savior*", "*Sin-Bearer*", "*Anointed One*", "*Only begotten Son*" and the "*Alpha and Omega*"(the first and last letters of the Greek alphabet). Dionysus is also thought to have turned water into wine. He was represented by the letters "IHS" and sometimes "IES".

The Celtic Druids and Gauls worshiped a person they called Esus or sometimes Hesus. He was believed to have been born on December 25th to a virgin as the son of the sun god and was the third person of the Celtic trinity. Hesus/Esus was believed to have been crucified with an elephant on one side and a lamb on the other. The elephant symbolizing the sins of the world and the lamb representing the innocence of Hesus/Esus. In some sense they believed "*the lamb of God took away the sins of the world*". The Celtic/Druid cross of Esus/Hesus which they worshiped remains popular to this day. The cross of Esus/Hesus was represented as an artistic cross made of interwoven branches on top of a circle, which symbolized the crucified son of the sun deity. Unfortunately many Christians mistake this Celtic/Druid cross as a Irish Christian cross and unknowingly wear them not knowing it's a cross of Esus/Hesus and not one of Jesus. When Julius Caesar conquered Gaul many Druids became roman slaves eventually gaining roman citizenship and their religion spread throughout the Roman Empire and is still practiced by some people today.

In Persia Zoroaster was called the "*Word made flesh*" and had a sacred cup teaching a religion that performed the Eucharist ritual. Allegedly born of a virgin, baptized in a river by "water, fire and holy wind", at 30 years of age he began his teaching, was tempted in the wilderness by the devil, cast demons out and reportedly gave sight to a blind man. While he is often depicted as one man it is more likely that there were many Zoroasters and they all conflated into one persona. The next Zoroaster is believed to come in 2341 CE and again be born to a virgin and begin his ministry at the age of 30.

Another deity of pagan Greece, Prometheus was called the "Logos"(Word) and had a fisherman friend known as "Petraeus"(Peter) who had deserted him. Prometheus was believed to have descended from heaven as God incarnated, he was thought to have been crucified and then risen from the dead in order to save mankind. When the pagan greeks performed their rituals they based their actions on the trinity. For instance they would sprinkle "holy water" on the altar 3 times and then sprinkle the people with it as well 3 times. Next they'd take some frankincense with three fingers and toss it upon the altar 3 times. This was done in accordance with what their oracle told them about all sacred things being done in threes.

In MesoAmerica the deity Quetzacoatl and his father Tezcatlipoca were believed to have killed the demon deity Cipatcli by pulling him apart in 4 directions, after distracting him by getting Cipatcli to eat the foot of Tezcatlipoca. The heaven was then made from the head of Cipatcli, earth made from his body and the underworld made from his tail. Then after the sacrifce of Tezcatlipoca's foot, Father and Son, created the Universe then Quetzacoatl came to earth as a human to be sacrificed for the salvation of all mankind. The Aztec and Mayan god Quetzalcoatl was believed to have been born of a virgin, tempted and fasted 40 days. Archaeological evidence suggests he had been crucified with nails driven through his hands and feet. Quetzalcoatl is sometimes represented as having been crucified between two thieves. Or with 3 crosses, a large cross in between two smaller crosses. After being crucified Quetzalcoatl is thought to have went to hell and rose from the dead on the third day before heading east. Mexican scriptures also depict Quetzalcoatl as having healed people, baptized, forgiven sins and been anointed with oil. A Eucharistic tradition also existed among Aztecs. Aztecs believed they ate the body of Quetzalcoatl in the form of a proxy, Aztecs were expecting his second coming when the Christian Spaniards invaded. One can imagine them arguing over religion, with the Christian shouting Jesus and the Aztec shouting Quetzalcoatl, both shoving crosses in each other's faces. Hernando Cortes, the Catholic Spanish conquistador who conquered the Aztecs, commented:

"the Devil had positively taught to the Mexicans the same things God had taught to Christendom." Incas and Aztecs also worshiped the "sun of God" thinking it would die if they didn't sacrifice people to it. Aztecs and Mayans who weren't killed by Spanish diseases or weapons eventually ended up converting to Christianity under the presumption that Quetzalcoatl and Christ were the same persons and that Christian rituals were just a different version of their pagan rites, some Aztecs even thought Cortez was Quetzalcoatl. The Spaniard's swords also provided them with extra motivation to become Christian too. After the Christianization process took place many books, monuments, artifacts and temples demonstrating the similarities between the mesoamerican religions and Christianity were destroyed or defaced. Although not all the evidence was destroyed and we are still able to know of the eerie similarities between Aztec and Christian beliefs. It is amazing how they held such similar beliefs despite Aztecs and early Christians not having contact with each other. It is a real shame that they don't teach the similarities between Aztec and Christian beliefs to kids in school when they teach children about the Aztecs. Although it's easy to guess why they don't, Aztec parents would probably complain.

     Attis of Phrygia was believed to have been born on December 25th. On "Black Friday" Attis was allegedly mutilated and bled to death under a pine tree. Believers in Attis thought he was the savior slain for the salvation of mankind who had his holy blood spilt for the redemption of the earth, who then descended into the underworld and rose again three days later. His festival took place during March 22-25th, a pine tree was cut on the 22nd and an image of Attis tied to the trunk, then the effigy was burned in a tomb. At night on March 24th priests opened the tomb and would conveniently find it empty to the astonishment of the crowd. On the 25th they celebrated the resurrection of Attis baptizing his followers in blood which caused their sins to be washed away, they were told they had been "born again" through Attis. Usually this would happen under a platform with the candidate standing in a pit where the blood of a bull would flow over them. The poor baptism candidates who couldn't afford to sacrifice a bull would use a sheep instead believing their sins were literally washed away by *"the blood of the lamb"*. The symbol of Astoria is the egg, which is part of the Easter egg tradition that people practice today. Thought of as being both the divine son and the father, the body of Attis was symbolically eaten in a ritual by his worshippers in the form of bread.

     The birthday of Jesus Christ was first celebrated by some churches in the spring and other churches celebrated it on January 6th. Orthodox Christians still celebrate it on January 6th to this day. There was significant confusion concerning the actual date of the birth of Jesus, even today no one knows the true date which the birth took place. Probably because Jesus never celebrated his own birthday anniversaries. In 345 CE

Pope Julius decreed that the birthday should thenceforth be held on December 25th, three days after the winter solstice, the same day on which the births of Mithras, Dionysus, Sol Invictus, Apollo, Attis, Dusares and several other pagan gods were celebrated. It was the most pagan day of the year and Pope Julius knew it. This means December 25th was the worst possible day he could have picked, unless he considered Christianity to be another pagan religion thinking that by celebrating the birth of Jesus on the same day as the pagans' celebrations it would make pagans more likely to convert to the Christian faith. But what's even worse than picking a pagan day to celebrate the unknown birthday was that most Christians at the time condemned birthday celebrations in total and didn't celebrate anybody's birthday, including their own, because they knew them to be a pagan religious ritual based on astrology, horoscopes, superstitions and the belief that a person had a special protector spirit/god since the day they were born and would throw a party for that god on the anniversary of their birthdate. Which of course since this spirit/god didn't exist the gifts were consumed by the pagan individual themselves. The popular Church father Origen even wrote that not only should Christians refrain from birthday celebrations but they should look upon their own birthdays with disgust. Although as baptism candles were given(and still are) which are meant to be lit on the anniversary of one's baptism, since pagans also used birthday candles for their superstitions and Christians considered baptism to be their "rebirth" eventually the Christians incorporated the pagan tradition of birthday candles with their baptismal candles. Doing this helped pagans who celebrated their birthdays convert to Christianity thinking they could still do their birthday parties, but could just call it a baptism party instead using the candle they got when baptised. Yet over time the baptismal candle tradition has been practically abandoned and now most Christians just do birthday celebrations exactly how the pagans did theirs. While Christians justify this by saying Jesus celebrated his birthday, which he didn't but even if they are referring to the Christmas story that's very different than the celebrations that get held today with entirely different rituals. Yet more importantly at best any celebration that may have took place when Jesus was born was a one day thing, they didn't do it every year. So doing it on the anniversary of your birth actually means such people think they are more important than Jesus since they claim he had one party in his life and they celebrate themselves once a year. The exception for Jesus is that his birth was divine miracle so that's actually something worth celebrating, once. Ours is not. Plus you know who's really special? Adam and Eve, they didn't have a "birthday" they had a "God created me" day, which they never celebrated annually because it's not an accomplishment of theirs and it doesn't please God.

    Not only would Paul be preaching something to sun cults, but also vegetation cults which were even older. Originally the king or leader of the tribe would be the sacrificial victim. Ancient man believed the prosperity of the tribe was dependent on the ruler's wellbeing. When the king became old or feeble, it was expected the tribe would suffer a similar decline. So the king, which they regarded as a god in human form, was sacrificed and then replaced. As their ideologies evolved instead of killing the king of the tribe they would substitute the son of the king to take his place in the sacrificial rite. The son being believed to be the offspring of divinity was called the "*son of god*". He was generally slain while tied to a sacred tree with arms outstretched in the shape of a cross. After that the body would be entombed and was thought to rise from the dead after three days, specifically three days because of the interval between the old and new moons. The moon was believed to have a direct correlation with the growth of crops. With the crop of wheat being made into bread which sustained the life of the world population. The bible references pagan Moabites killing the firstborn son of their king in a battle with Israelites thinking the sacrifice would grant them salvation from defeat in 2 Kings 3:26-27, "*When the king of Moab saw that the battle had gone against him, he took with him seven hundred swordsmen to break through to the king of Edom, but they failed.* ²⁷ **Then he took his firstborn son, who was to succeed him as king, and offered him as a sacrifice on the city wall.** *The fury against Israel was great; they withdrew and returned to their own land.*"

  The English translation of the New International Version of the bible also says God hates sons being sacrificed and it's a practice of disbelievers to kill their kids in 2 Kings 16:2-4, "*Ahaz was twenty years old when he became king, and he reigned in Jerusalem sixteen years.* **Unlike David his father, he did not do what was right** *in the eyes of the Lord his God.* ³ *He followed the ways of the kings of Israel and* **even sacrificed his son in the fire, engaging in the detestable practices of the nations the Lord had driven out before the Israelites.** ⁴ *He offered sacrifices and burned incense at the high places, on the hilltops and under every spreading tree.*" These verses also indicate that David did what was right in the view of God thereby clearing him of the slander other parts of the bible contain accusing him of adultery. They also inform us that burning incense as an act of worship is another thing God detests. Yet today many Christians burn incense in church as part of their worship services. While the bible continues to tell another instance of what Jews did that caused God to hate them in 2 Kings 21:1-16, "*Manasseh was twelve years old when he became king, and he reigned in Jerusalem fifty-five years. His mother's name was Hephzibah.* ² **He did evil in the eyes of the Lord, following the detestable practices of the nations the Lord had driven out before the Israelites.** ³ **He rebuilt the high places his father Hezekiah had destroyed; he also erected altars to Baal and made an Asherah pole**, *as Ahab king of Israel had done.* **He bowed down to all the starry hosts and worshiped them.** ⁴ **He built altars in the temple of the Lord**, *of which the Lord had said, "In Jerusalem I will put my Name."* ⁵ *In the two courts of the temple of the Lord, he built altars to all the starry hosts.* ⁶ *He sacrificed his own son in the fire, practiced divination, sought omens, and consulted mediums and spiritists. He did much* *evil in the eyes of the Lord, arousing his anger. ⁷He took the carved Asherah pole he had made and put it in the temple, of which the Lord had said to David and to his son Solomon, "In this temple and in Jerusalem, which I have chosen out of all the tribes of Israel, I will put my Name forever. ⁸I will not again make the feet of the Israelites wander from the land I gave their ancestors, if only they will be careful to do everything I commanded them and will keep the whole Law that my servant Moses gave them." ⁹But the people did not listen. Manasseh led them astray, so that **they did more evil than the nations the Lord had destroyed** before the Israelites. ¹⁰**The Lord said through his servants the prophets:** ¹¹"Manasseh king of Judah has committed **these detestable sins.** He has done more evil than the Amorites who preceded him and has led Judah into sin with his idols. ¹²Therefore this is what the Lord, the God of Israel, says: I am going to bring such disaster on Jerusalem and Judah that the ears of everyone who hears of it will tingle. ¹³I will stretch out over Jerusalem the measuring line used against Samaria and the plumb line used against the house of Ahab. I will wipe out Jerusalem as one wipes a dish, wiping it and turning it upside down. ¹⁴I will forsake the remnant of my inheritance and give them into the hands of enemies. They will be looted and plundered by all their enemies; ¹⁵they have done evil in my eyes and have aroused my anger from the day their ancestors came out of Egypt until this day." ¹⁶Moreover, Manasseh also shed so much innocent blood that he filled Jerusalem from end to end – besides the sin that he had caused Judah to commit, so that they did evil in the eyes of the Lord."*

This passage highlights specific acts of pagan worship the Israelites copied which God hates with a passion. Rebuilding pagan places was detested. Making altars to Baal and an Asherah pole was also detestable. As was building altars in temples in general. Yet Christians are famous for altars in churches, and Christian scholars even say that the altars started out being built as tombs over martyrs. Thus the graves of Christian martyrs were made into places of worship, as the Vatican is believed to be built on the graves of Peter and Paul. Regarding Baal many pagans used the word "Baal", which means "Lord", to describe their god but there is a specific type of Baal which is referenced here that God detests, verse 3 tells us Manasseh erected altars to the same Baal that Ahab had done. According to the bible Ahab had married a famous disbeliever called Jezebel who worshiped a Baal who was considered the son of El and had been killed and resurrected from the dead. The word El was short for Elohim, which was a name for the Creator of everything, so the Baal Jezebel worshiped was an alleged son of the true God who they thought was killed and rose from the dead. While the Asherah pole was a phallic pole or obelisk; similar to the phallic Washington Monument and the obelisk outside the Vatican in St. Peter's Square. The key difference between Asherah poles and regular phallic obelisks was that pagans put sunbursts on top of the Asherah poles. They were essentially sun pillars where people gathered to worship the Sun of God likely combining it with the phallic pagan obelisks to emphasize how just as when an erect penis "dies" or loses it's erection after intercourse thereby giving life as a result, the

Sun of God also died at the vernal equinox so that they could have eternal life and they would rejoice everyday when the Sun of God rose again over the phallic pillar stirring them to daily exuberance and excitement akin to the excitement an erect penis causes. Since the penis didn't stay erect forever it meant humans wouldn't live forever as life given by man was temporary, but because the sun pillar or Asherah pole stayed erect 24/7 and the sun would always shine it's light on the pole and those around it, they took it to mean that the "Sun of God" provides eternal life only to those who worship it around the Asherah pole. God is said to have immensely detested the Israelites' worshipping the numerous "Baals" of the polytheistic pagans in the English translation of the New International Version of the Bible in Judges 2:11-13,

"Then <u>the Israelites did evil in the eyes of the Lord and served the Baals.</u> *12 They forsook the Lord, the God of their ancestors, who had brought them out of Egypt. They followed and worshiped various gods of the peoples around them. They aroused the Lord's anger 13 because they forsook him and served Baal and the Ashtoreths."*

And in Judges 3:1-7, *"These are the nations the Lord left to test all those Israelites who had not experienced any of the wars in Canaan 2 (he did this only to teach warfare to the descendants of the Israelites who had not had previous battle experience): 3 the five rulers of the Philistines, all the Canaanites, the Sidonians, and the Hivites living in the Lebanon mountains from Mount Baal Hermon to Lebo Hamath. 4 <u>They were left to test the Israelites to see whether they would obey the Lord's commands, which he had given their ancestors through Moses.</u> 5 The Israelites lived among the Canaanites, Hittites, Amorites, Perizzites, Hivites and Jebusites. 6 They took their daughters in marriage and gave their own daughters to their sons, and served their gods. 7<u>**The Israelites did evil in the eyes of the Lord; they forgot the Lord their God and served the Baals and the Asherahs.**</u>"*

Keep in mind those who worshiped Baal still believed that God had created everything. The problem was they attributed a son to God which he never had and claimed their Baal or that the son of God was the Lord instead of God. The way God uses the word "Baals" in the bible indicates that he didn't distinguish between one Baal and the other, they were all false deities that were alleged to be his sons. A misconception is that all pagan idolatry involved worshipping statues. While it is idolatrous to have statues, most pagans who worshiped these Baals considered the statue to be a powerless representation of the alleged son of God whom they were praying to. So when the bible says serving Baals was evil idolatry, it's not simply because the pagans had statues of Baals. The idolatry was the fact that they falsely attributed sons to God and prayed to them instead of God alone. The bible explains that Israelites fell into this polytheism by marrying disbelievers which led them and their children to believe in alleged sons of God which God never had. Thus they forgot that they should only pray to God and no others besides him, as the first commandment instructed. The

Israelites didn't forget the commandment itself, they just distorted it's meaning and didn't follow it as Moses taught them to. Some likely just used Baal as an intercessor, thinking he wasn't God but that Baal would pray to God on their behalf if they prayed to Baal. To God this was disbelief. But it gets even worse as verse 7 indicates they also served Asherahs. This is not to be confused with Asherah poles which have already been explained. Asherah herself was thought of as a consort to El or Elohim/Yahweh/God. Also referred to as the "Queen of Heaven". Which ironically enough is the same exact title which Catholics and some Eastern Orthodox Christians give for Mary the mother of Jesus. They also claim that Mary is the "Mother of God", since they consider her son Jesus to be God their Lord and Savior. Whereas Asherah was considered the mother of Baal. When the bible condemns people serving Baals and Asherahs, it is a condemnation of all the false religions that teach God has kids or consorts. The prophets Elijah and Elisha condemned these evil beliefs and practices as idolatry and the bible says they killed those guilty of such crimes.

That covers some of the sun cults which existed and historically contaminated the Israelites' beliefs causing God to hate them, but there were also other religions practiced at the time Paul started preaching his message.

The Buddhist priests of Tibet are called Lamas. The Grand Lama (Dalai Lama) is believed to be the direct successor to the Saint La having the actual soul of Saint La within him and acts as Supreme Pontiff, who is thought to be immaculate and infallible just as Roman Catholics believe the Pope is. The Dalai Lama is thought to have the power to bless people and is considered the vicegerent of God whose interpretation of sacred books is thought to be divine inspiration, once more just like what Roman Catholics believe about the Pope. When a French Jesuit missionary named Father Evariste Régis Huc visited the Lamas in Tibet he saw their religion included: "Holy water", prayers for the dead, singing in their services, relics of their saints, the burning of incense, monasteries and convents, monks who chant, fasting and prayer beads as well. Vajra Buddhism even has a baptismal rite of initiation! Then the Jesuit missionary tried to persuade the Buddhists to become Roman Catholic. After the Catholic missionary finished his lengthy explanation of Catholicism, the Tibetan lama famously replied: *Your religion is the same as ours*." Now what people typically don't know is that Buddha is a title referring to "one who is awake" and is a state of mind, not a name. The title of Buddha doesn't necessarily refer to the most famous Buddha Siddhārtha Gautama. Buddhists believe in 28 confirmed Buddhas, Gautama being the most recent, although more than 28 are believed to have existed. There are many different Buddhas and forms of Buddhism. Some Buddhists even believe in one Buddha who was crucified, died and resurrected who had been nailed through his hands and feet. Of course not all denominations of Buddhism believe this, but there are Sanskrit texts which teach that this other Buddha had 12 disciples, was thought to be divine and taught baptism in the name of Buddha, the Dharma and the Samgha. Another little known fact about Buddhism is that Buddhists believe in a trinity, but it is difficult to explain and understand since the many different Buddhist branches have different names for the parts of it and exactly what/who it is. One narration of a Buddha has him say, "*Enough, Vakkali. Why do you want to see this filthy body? Whoever sees the Dhamma sees me; whoever sees me sees the Dhamma.*" Some Buddhists think this statement confirms that particular Buddha's divinity in that he and the Dhamma are one and the Buddha is part of the trinity. Coincidentally this is nearly identical to the bible verse which claims Jesus said whoever sees him has seen the father although the Buddhist record predates the gospel verse. Professor Soothill has even recorded that he heard Buddhist children in India singing "*Buddha loves me, this I know. For the Sutras tell me so.*" which is nearly identical to the Christian lyrics to a popular hymn/song except Christian's replace the word Buddha with Jesus and Sutras with Bible. On most key points concerning morality, Buddhism and Christianity are nearly identical and in complete agreement. Therefore when we look deep into Catholicism and Buddhism it makes total sense for the Tibetan Lama to have told the Jesuit missionary that "*Your religion is the same as ours.*" Since Buddhism is much older than Christianity some have claimed Christianity is a copycat, but personally I don't think Paul or early Christians came into contact with Buddhism or were directly influenced by Buddhist doctrines. Although Buddhism was purportedly studied and practiced in Egypt during the time of Jesus. The cultural center of Alexandria, which was an interfaith melting pot, was even a learning center for many early Christian leaders. Yet since writing developed in China, Central America, Egypt and Mesopotamia all independently and simultaneously around 3,000 BCE, the similarities could all be coincidental.

     In India Krishna is said to have had his birth heralded by a bright star, descending from royal lineage he was humbly born in a cave and visited by wise men and shepherds as an infant; thousands of years before Jesus. King Kansa ordered the killing of all male children born on the same night as Krishna in an attempt to kill the boy, but his parents were warned by angels to flee to safety. Krishna was believed to be "without sin" who was both a human and divine son of God, as well as God incarnated who came to earth to cleanse human beings of all sins. Titles for Krishna included: "*Redeemer*", "*Son of God*", "*Firstborn*", "*Universal Word*", "*Sin-Bearer*" and "*Our Lord and Saviour*". Hindus also burn incense in their temples. Those who wash with sacred water before entering the Hindu temple are thought to have all their sins washed away and are "born again". A Hindu Brahmin who did the half-month sacrifices regularly was thought to become a god for that time-frame. To transition from being mortal to being immortal they were sprinkled with water to symbolize a seed. Then they pretended to be an embryo by being shut up in a special hut symbolizing the womb. Under their robe would be a belt and black antelope skin to represent the inner and outer membranes an embryo is wrapped in. While pretending to be an embryo they couldn't scratch themselves with nails or sticks, because if an embryo were scratched with such things it would die. If they moved in the hut it was because embryos move in the womb, if the fists were clenched it was because embryo's fists are clenched in the womb as well. If while bathing they took off the antelope skin but kept the robe on it was because the child is born with the inner membrane but not the outer. After this embryo stage the Brahmin was "born again" as a god on earth. In modern India these "born again" ceremonies are for sinners who become a new person after expiation, no longer thinking themselves to be responsible for the sins they committed in their earlier state. Aborigines of India punish criminals with a "born-again" ceremony where the guilty is put in a sealed earthen pot, buried in the sand and comes out as a fresh incarnation of earth. However then they are put in a grass hut that is burned and they run out as it burns to get immersed in water, afterward they get their hair cut and pay a fee. Thereby they are "born-again" as a new person and free from all responsibility for the previous crimes they committed. There are other hindu "born again" ceremonies as well that involve rituals similar to baptism, and those who do them have a similar attitude as "born again" Christians. The Hindu deity Krishna was known as "the lion of the tribe of Saki" in contrast to Jesus being known as "the lion of the tribe of Judah". While by a tree, Krishna is said to have been pierced by an arrow the force of which nailed him to it causing him to die, although some statues show both his hands and feet having been pierced and other statues show actual nails in his hands and feet with his side being pierced too. The light of the sun is said to have been blotted out at noon on the day Krishna died while the sky rained fire and ashes. Then Krishna is believed to have risen from the dead as he had prophesied and many allegedly witnessed him ascend to heaven. If one doesn't believe in the divinity of Krishna, his resurrection and status as the savior of the world, then it is thought that person will be in hell forever whereas those who believe Krishna died for their sins will be forgiven and enjoy paradise forever. The second person in the Hindu trinity is Krishna. Their trinity consists of Brahma, Vishnu and Siva Krishna with Krishna being considered as the human incarnation of Vishnu. Hindus believe in the concept of purgatory just like Catholics. Hinduism is well known as a polytheist religion, yet most Christians believe in a trinity just like Hindus and have other striking similarities but consider themselves monotheist.

    The mystery of the trinity is solved when its origins are examined. The word trinity itself does not occur in the entire bible one time, so belief in it has no basis from the bible at all. The Greek pagan philosopher Plato promoted belief in a trinity in his Phaedon written in 400 BCE. Plato taught the trinity was "*Agathon, Logos and Psyche*" which translated from Greek means "*The Father, the Word and the Spirit*". "St." Augustine had said he found the beginning of John's Gospel in Plato's Phaedon, which is an admission of the similarities between pagan doctrine and Christian doctrine and a potential admission of copying. An ancient pagan obelisk at Rome had a Greek inscription which said, "*1. The Mighty God. 2. The Begotten God. 3. Apollo the Spirit.*" The famous Christian authority "Saint" Jerome himself even stated, "*All the ancient nations believed in the trinity.*" Which is rather self-condemning because most of the ancient nations are considered to be polytheistic pagans with Jews being the only monotheists known of from ancient times. If polytheist pagans of old believed in a trinity, wouldn't that mean belief in a trinity is a form of polytheism? Pagan trinities also depicted the second part of the trinity as being begotten by the first part. Surely the belief in a trinity cannot be a divinely revealed doctrine if heathens were practicing it long beforehand. If so then it would mean the pagans had the right idea about God all along and their pagan faith was based on divine revelation. Either the pagans were divinely inspired long before Trinitarian Christians or neither of these groups were. The early Church father Justin Martyr remarked on the similarities between Pagan and Christian doctrines in his "First Apology", which was an apologetic evangelical work in which he wrote: "*And when we say also that the Word, who is the first-birth of God, was produced without sexual union, and that He, Jesus Christ, our Teacher, was crucified and died, and rose again, and ascended into heaven, we propound nothing different from what you believe regarding those whom you esteem sons of Jupiter...*" According to Justin Martyr, Christianity was "*nothing different*" from what the pagan polytheists believed. In the sight of this famous early Christian scholar of antiquity the Christian doctrine wasn't strange, new, or unheard of.

Another pagan god Mithra/Mithras was alleged to have been born to a virgin named Anahita in a cave on December 25th. Believed to be the second person of a holy trinity both human and divine, his human mother was titled "*the Mother of God*". On January 6th there would be a reenactment of the Persian magi who came to worship the baby Mithras while he was still in the cradle, the magi brought frankincense, gold and myrrh as gifts to the newborn god in keeping with the pagan tradition that these three things are to be used when worshipping a god. Other denominations of this religion depict him as being born out of a rock as a god in human form, without mother or father making him the direct indisputable "*son of God*". This was probably a misunderstanding taken out of context by misinterpretations of Mithraic scriptures which say he was born in a cave, interpreters and translators could have easily made "born in a cave" into "born of a rock" by mistake. His earliest worshippers were shepherds, it is thought he had 12 companions who would accompany him learning what he taught. He was known as: "*the Light of the World*", "*the Way, the Truth, the Light*", "*the Life*", "*the Word*", "*the Son of God*", "*the Redeemer*", "*the Savior*", "*the Logos*" and "*the Good Shepherd*". He was considered to be a mediator between heaven and earth, and his worshippers were called "soldiers of Mithra". Mithras was believed to have healed the sick and raised the dead. Mithras is believed to have said: "*He who will not eat of my body and drink of my blood, so that he will be made one with me and I with him, the same shall not know salvation.*"

Mithraists did this by drinking wine and eating bread which represented the body and blood of Mithras, doing this gave them a reputation for being cannibals. The followers of Mithras were baptized in water naked and would then put on a white gown thinking their sins had been washed away. The rituals of the worshippers of Mithras took place on Sunday, which since Mithras was considered "the Lord" the worshippers of Mithras called Sunday "the Lord's day". Ancient sites of Mithraic worship have been found in many places of the world including: Britain, Italy, Romania, Germany, Hungary, Bulgaria, Turkey, Persia, Armenia, Syria, Israel, India, China and North Africa. The Christian "Saint" Augustine went so far as to say that Mithraists worshiped the same God he did, citing how both Mithraists and Catholics had 7 sacraments which were basically the same. The early Church father Tertullian commented on the popular Mithraic faith by saying, *"The priests of Mithras promised absolution from sin on confession and baptism."* Mithraic priests would even lay hands on confirmation candidates in the same manner as I had experienced when I was confirmed as a Catholic. As a former Catholic, while not having as much authority as Tertullian or "St." Augustine, I can personally testify that there are very few differences between Mithraic and Catholic doctrines and practices. The major difference is that Mithras isn't believed to have been crucified. Instead Mithra/Mithras is believed to have slaughtered a large bull whose blood was accepted as atonement for the sins of the world. Any Mithraist who believed Mithra/Mithras had made the sacrifice and worshiped him as the son of God thinking Mithra/Mithras obtained the salvation of man, by spilling the blood of a mighty bull, thought eternal paradise awaited them with eternal hellfire awaiting the non-Mithraists. The depiction of this event includes many other animals in the scene and rich imagery too detailed to describe here, but each thing represented has symbolic correlation with the zodiac or some other thing of pagan spiritual significance. Some even believe the depiction of the bull being slaughtered by Mithra/Mithras is representative of him sacrificing himself as an atonement for sins, since he was also known as *"the great bull of the Sun"*. The sacrifice was followed by a Last Supper that Mithras had with his companions where they dined before Mithras ascended to heaven having accomplished his sacrificial mission, later to return to combat the forces of evil. Since this sacrifice includes extensive symbolism I doubt it is an accurate portrayal of any historical event, it was probably specifically depicted because of its symbolism without any basis from an actual sacrifice. It is noteworthy that the depiction of the sacrifice is always in a cave, which was symbolic of the world and the victory of Mithras. The success of his sacrifice is depicted with him leaving the cave surrounded by light. The religion of Mithras was practiced by many people throughout the Roman Empire long before Jesus was born. More than a hundred inscriptions dedicated to Mithras have been discovered in Rome, along with 75 sculpture fragments, and a series of Mithraic temples situated in all parts of the city. Of course it was well known that Rome wasn't always Catholic, but the majority of people today don't know it use to be a spiritual center of the pagan Mithraic religion. The Mithraists also had a "*pope who always lived at Rome*" and called him "Papa" or "Pontifus Maximus", while ordinary worship leaders were called "*fathers*". If Christianity was at one time divinely inspired then how come so many of the "divinely inspired" rituals originated in a pagan religion? Does that mean the worshippers of Mithras were also divinely inspired? What is even more disturbing is that the Mithraic scholars traced the origin of their pagan religion of Mithras to have first started in the city of Tarsus in Cilicia. This Tarsus is the same city Saul/Paul was born in. Saul/Paul would've known about this pagan religion since birth and had been at the epicenter of the Mithraic world. Therefore Saul needed to change his name to Paul because being known as "Saul of Tarsus" would have led people to think he was just preaching the religion of his hometown. People still practice this pagan religion today, openly saying they worship Mithras claiming that Catholics and Christians stole their religious practices and ideas. Mithraism was so popular in ancient Rome that in 307 CE the roman emperor proclaimed Mithra to be the "protector of the empire". In the fourth century the roman emperor Julian, who was raised Christian, left Christianity and adopted Mithraism establishing temples devoted to Mithras at Constantinople. In 362 CE Julian proclaimed the Roman Empire would have freedom of religion and Mithraism remained a serious contender and rival to Christianity. Considering that the Jewish and Christian people knew of this pagan religion and rejected Paul's teachings casts extreme doubt on his claims of divine inspiration. Saul/Paul himself even admits that no Christians or Jews followed him, so he taught gentile pagans the "truth about Jesus" and it was accepted by them. Saul persecuted the followers of Jesus then changed his name to Paul and taught religion in Greek, a language Jesus never spoke, which Jesus' followers didn't know to be able to refute any of Paul's teachings due to the language barrier. Many pagans already practiced most of what Saul/Paul was teaching, a transition from pagan religions to Paul's religion would have been easy to make. Now we will cover the snake cult beliefs.

Ancient Egyptians used the Ouroborus as a symbol of the sun and Gnostics used it as a symbol of the sun god Abraxas and the symbol of the "soul of the world". The Ouroborus is greek for "tail swallower" and is depicted as a snake eating it's own tail. There is a dragon version as well.

Many cultures besides the Egyptians and Greeks believed in Ouroborus, such as the the Norse, the Native Americans and others. The Gnostic text Pistis Sophia states the sun of God is a 12 part dragon biting it's own tail in Ouroborus, which is why we have a 12 hour clock that eternally repeats 12 hours by 12 hours by 12 hours and why they say Jesus was crucified at 12 o'clock noon since that is the key turning point and time which the "O" Ouroborus does it deed that results in eternal life. Sometimes Ouroborus is a circular snake/dragon symbol which is where the phrase *"the circle of life"* comes from. Other times it is depicted as an 8 type of symbol which is where the mathmatical infinity symbol ∞ comes from. This snake symbol represented eternal life.

Yet the eight-like shaped Ouroborus symbol is specially symbolic because it expands upon the original "O" Ouroborus. The original plain circle Ouroborus snake head meant chaos while the middle section meant peace with the end meaning chaos once again where the self-eating took place. With the eight-like Ouroborus snake eating taking place in the middle/center then this showed a different outlook on time and led to different religious doctrines. No longer did the pagan outlook view history as chaos-peace-chaos and repeat, but instead there would be 2 parts of history with the eternal sacrifice taking place once in the middle without any identifiable beginning or end. Yet since there had to be a beginning and since the beginning started with the head of the snake/dragon but the snake sacrifice occured at the middle of the timeline this meant that even though the sacrifice took place in the middle the snake existed on both sides having existed before and after their sacrifice which results in eternal infinite life. Hence the pagan saviour religions incorporated this revised vision of time to suggest their pagan sacrificial saviours also existed before and after their sacrifices with their sacrifices having been the very reason they were created.

Wedding rings also originate from this idea of marriage being an eternal self-sacrifice of survival for which it was thought that if 2 people get matching "O" Ouroborus rings then they will eternally live happy ever after. This mutual survival factor is better demonstrated in the twin opposite colored snake co-Ouroborus depictions which were also influenced by dualist theologies and symbols like the famous oriental yin yang. If you notice the double snake Ouroborus is knotted up in the middle, anatomically that is a mess however it wasn't knotted just to be fancy. For pagans religion and magic were intertwined with magic being a part of their religions, pagans believed in magic rather than miracles and used spells instead of sacraments. Regarding their magical spells knots were one method used by magicians to work their magic. As such the Ouroborus was a popular magical symbol which people would frequently use to write spells inside of.

This is also why getting married and putting the rings on one's spouse is called "tying the knot". The rings were thought to have magical powers that could keep the couple who wore the rings together for eternity. This was because the Egyptians said rings were "without beginning or end" so they were seen as prime tools for eternally binding magic. Afterall haven't you seen the pictures where 2 rings are connected to each other, just like the double snake Ouroborus, that's an allusion to the magical bond of the rings. Wedding rings were idolatrous magical amulets. As such the pagan priests had to officiate marriages and perform the ceremonies in which the "knot was tied", since the priests were the ones who knew how to do the magic to make the rings work. Incorrectly some think "tying the knot" refers to ropes being involved in some cultural weddings, which it is true there were some magical rope tying traditions where the couple would be tied together, but "tying the knot" just meant to "do the magic" and applied to magic in general rather than ropes or rope magic specifically. The left hand was used because that was the "sinister" hand, (sinister originally meant left). Magicians believe in 2 types of magic, black hand magic and white hand magic, these are also called the "left hand path" and the "right hand path" even though both paths are wrong and lead to the hellfire. Although to be completely honest the term "path" is a modern phrase and ancient pagans called it "way" instead of "path" so black magic was really known as the "left hand way". It is because black magic is seen as taboo by magicians that the "left hand way" was seen as bad and left handed people were viewed as evil in the ancient past. Magicians themselves have such views of black magic because it is more malicious and does not follow ethical morality, an example being love magic which forces someone to love another against their will. Since the wedding ring ouroborus love magic was a type of black magic they used the left hand for the wedding ring and not the right hand. Unfortunately the Christians built upon this pagan wedding ring magic by specifying the left index finger as the "ring finger". Some say Christians did this thinking the left index finger has a vein which leads to the heart. When getting married Christians would invoke the trinity to work the magic in their marriage by raising their left hand and Saying "In the name of the Father,(for their thumb), In the name of the Son (for their pointer finger), In the name of the Holy Spirit "(for their middle finger) and then they'd seal the spell by putting the ring on the 4th finger which had the vein leading to the heart which would hopefully send the magic to the heart emotionally permanently magically binding the couple forever or as long as they wore the rings. It depended on how seriously the Christian believed in it and how effective the magic actually was. Despite magic being forbidden this is what the superstitious early and medieval Christians did and some still do such at Royal weddings to this very day. But the alleged "vein of love" that leads to the heart isn't even in that ring finger, it's actually in the middle finger. Which is why giving one the middle finger is considered so offensive because the vein goes right to the heart, so when you "flip someone off" the blood used is literally coming directly from the heart without detours. Yet all of these dumb pagans and Christians were doing love magic putting wedding rings on the wrong finger and they still do it to this day on that same finger! They shouldn't be using the rings at all, because magic is evil but because of scientific stupidity they do it wrong according to their own beliefs anyways. So it's funny but not funny at the same time, because the rings are bad. However why do they really use the left index finger to this day, when it's known that finger's vein doesn't lead to the heart? This is because the left hand index finger is also known as "the left finger" because it is to the left of the middle finger on the left hand and the pinky is shorter and there are debates whether the pinky counts as a finger. So using the left index finger was like far left "left hand way". For black magic that was the most magical finger, or so they thought. Thus that is why that finger was used and is still used today, because the rings were supposed to be tools of love magic. Furthermore to make the magic extra potent certain metals would be used, like gold, and the rings would be engraved with spells written on them. Since the rings were the most potent part of the magical ritual a special position of a "ring bearer" was made whose job it was to carry both rings during the ceremony until the time came for them to be given to the couple so the magic could bind them. Christians still have this magical ring-bearer job today, but usually get a cute little child to do it, he carries the rings on a pillow because the love magic also contains some sex magic and the rings on the pillow is sexually symbolic. The Christian marriage ritual is practically the same today with all the specific ceremonial steps, once believed to be vital for the magic, in which the spouses to be must recite certain phrases at the behest of their mage/minister with customary vows being sworn on the spot as well, finally closing with the couples saying "I do" and "sealing the deal" by "tying the knot" and swapping saliva when they kiss thereafter. This kiss was a way of tying a knot with your tongue which the teeth can't untie. Hence whenever a person got nervous doing the vows and had trouble saying them they were accused of being "tongue tied". It was believed the reason they had trouble saying the magical wedding spells was because they were already magically married to someone else and the magic wouldn't let their tongue tie a magical knot of marriage with another person. Which of course such scandalous speculations only increased the anxiety such a stutterer might have making it even harder for them to speak, which only confirmed the pagan superstitions especially if the accused fainted under pressure. If someone were to be "tongue tied" while trying to say the wedding rites that could end up cancelling a wedding and preventing a marriage. The Christian marriage rite was identical to the magical pagan rite except they just invoked different deitites/holy spirits or holy ghosts. Shamefully most of the magical elements of Christian, and by extension Western weddings, remain without the masses being aware that they are performing pagan magical religious practices when they get married. Flower Bouguets were made with strong scents to frighten away evil spirits and that's why wedding parties would have flower boys and flower girls casting flowers out on the ground before the wedding procession. This is also why each member of the bridal parties would wear a flower on their person for spiritual protection. The power of flowers would also be used in the home when preparing a trail of flowers leading to the bed to protect the couple from evil spirits who may interfere with their sexual relations. Today most people think it's "romantic" to lay a flower petal trail to the bed instead of knowing it's flower power magic. After the wedding the flower bouquet would be tossed to transfer the luck of the bride to someone else. Brides would frequently braid their hairs tying magical knots hoping for fertility as a result. Rice and Nuts would be thrown on the new couple to ensure they had a bountiful harvest, but because churches hated cleaning up rice afterward they lied to people saying birds exploded when they eat rice in the hopes people would stick to throwing just nuts. Although nuts were eventually seen as too sexually suggestive so few people throw nuts today. Bells would be rung loudly to drive evil spirits away, church bells were later invented for this reason and that is why they were rung hour after hour and during thunderstorms. Brides would wear "something old, something new, something borrowed and something blue" to their wedding. The old thing was to benefit from magic used in the previous bride's marriage, the borrowed thing would be taken from a women blessed with children to induce fertility, the something new would be to transfer the old magic and old fertility to the new bride, while the something blue was thought to protect against the evil eye which could cause infertility. "A silver sixpence in her shoe" was a British custom later invented and added to the rhyme to induce wealth and prosperity. Other foolish customs to avoid the evil eye would be that the bride could not wear her wedding dress before the day, nor look at herself while wearing her dress in the mirror, nor could the groom see the bride the day of the wedding until the ceremony lest it cause evil eye that prevents the marriage or causes a curse to befall them. Since the fear of evil spirits was so great a tradition of bridesmaids and groom's mates was invented where friends/sisters of the bride and friends/brothers of the groom dress up as decoys for the evil spirits to attack should such spirits try to stop the wedding. Christians still do this today, with modern assistants considering it an honor not knowing they are supposed to be making themselves decoy targets for devils. Because of all the magical rituals that had to be done a tradition of "wedding rehearsals" began which was a rehearsal for the magical ritual so everyone would stand in the right spots and the ritual would be completed flawlessly so the magic would be most potent. People still do these wedding rehearsals today, "to get the steps right" not knowing the whole point of "getting everything right" was because the wedding itself was a magical ritual. Thus if you aren't doing magic you don't need to rehearse anything, but they do these rehearsals anyways because they truly do want a "magical wedding" even if they don't desire magic to be done. This is also why bridal showers and male "stag parties" were done. Before the wedding brides would be "showered" with gifts and incantations in the hopes that they'd be gifted with a magical wedding, this was also done for "baby showers" in the hopes that showering expectant mothers with gifts and incantations would ensure magical protection for the child and mother.

Whereas the male groom's "stag party" was designed as a hunt where the groom to be would go out and commit acts of sexual debauchery to trick the evil spirits into thinking he was not getting married the next day because nobody in love about to get married would act like that. The infamous stag parties were incorporated with fertilization cult orgies to give the man one last time to fornicate before being magically bound to his wife. Wedding candles or lanterns would be lit to send the couple's wishes for their marriage into the sky to the gods. Wedding cakes were made to induce fertility and broken over the bride's head to make her fertile, today the couple shoves cake in each other's faces thinking it's funny or romantic instead of magic. While to make both people fertile the couple would kiss over the cake, but since the families wanted lots of fertility they made bigger and bigger cakes stacking them higher and higher until they got so big that the couple couldn't stand over the cake to kiss. So how did they solve this magic cake dilemma? They made voodoo statues of the couple and put the magical voodoo statues of the couple on top of the cake. This is why wedding cakes have little plastic representations of the bride and groom, it was a type of pagan fertility voodo. Yet since the couple could no longer eat the cake themselves a tradition of distributing the cake began so that the family as a whole would magically increase their fertility. While the couple walking under arches was also thought to have magical effects and a greeting line was made to lead the couple out protecting them on either side from any evil spirits who might attack before the wedding magic took complete effect. Pagans would lead the couple to their quick mode of transportation which would have noisemakers attached to it so that while they traveled away from the ceremony the noise would ward off any evil spirits who may be in pursuit so that way they could escape the spirits indefinitely. Today this is usually done by the couple putting strings with tin cans on the back of the car, which was started to have the noise of the tin cans frighten evil spirits. Most all the traditions in the Christian wedding rites are sinful and on top of that the wedding rings are overpriced scams, so it wasn't even cheap magic when they did it in the past but today they do the same rituals except they don't even believe in it. So as stupid as the pagans were, those doing it today are even dumber because they don't even know why they do what they do, they just blush when they say "I do" while they don't have a clue of the amount of spiritual trouble they've gotten themselves into; all in the name of " traditions". Even with the popular fictional "Lord of the Rings" series alluding to the magical beliefs and potential rings can have, the masses never seem to connect the dots and realize wedding rings and engagement rings are bad things. In the ancient world the pagans would wear "oath rings". An oath ring was typically golden or silver and sometimes they were engraved. Frequently an "oath ring" would be dipped in blood, sometimes the blood of the "oath taker", prior to them swearing an oath with the ring and then putting the ring onto their finger as a way of binding them to their oath. Then they'd keep the "oath ring" on until they fulfilled their oath thinking the ring made them fulfill it more easily or would cause them harm if they failed to fulfill their oath or remove it. As "oath rings" became popular people got fancy with them thinking the bigger an oath was the bigger a ring it required, so they made "wrist rings" which were much akin to modern bracelets. The "wrist rings" were then upgraded to "neck rings" both of which served the same purpose as "oath rings" but they were more expensive and visible than the "oath rings" were. Those who wanted people who saw them to know about their oath wouldn't get a plain "oath ring", but opted for a "wrist ring" or "neck ring" so people knew how important their oath was to them. Today instead of "wrist rings" and "neck rings" worn for magical oaths people wear bracelets and necklaces/chains for "fashion". Of course not every pagan could afford to buy a "neck ring" or a "wrist ring" to show off all their oaths, plus poor people suspected many were upgrading their "oath rings" just to show they were rich. So rather than admit they were arrogant in their oaths new doctrines were developed regarding "oath rings" specifying that certain oaths needed particular rings. Thus neck rings symbolized how one's neck was on the line for that oath or wrist rings could be a promise of one's hand being pledged to service to king, tribe, owner etc. Anklets could be used to show how one's ability to travel was conditional and free movement was not something they had. Meanwhile other oaths could be body part specific. For example an earring could symbolize one's oath not to listen to certain people or types of speech, while a lip ring could denote restrictions on eating, a tongue ring could represent restrictions on speech and a nose ring could signify restrictions on smell. In short most types of jewelry worn today began as magical spells and/or were worn as a result of taking a very serious oath. The jewelry could denote one's limitations on liberty or their special rights depending on the particular individual's cultural/religious beliefs. Another effect of this "oath ring" phenomenon is that because it was expensive to get the extravagant jewelry type of "oath rings" then rich people naturally had more "oath rings" of various types and this gave them a reputation in society for taking more oaths and being more trustworthy since their oaths were more visible than the pagan peasant's plain "oath ring" for the finger. This has continued to distort the mentality of the masses in modern times so that the wealthy are regarded as more honest or trustworthy than the poor. Meanwhile oath rings are still used today for many different reasons, some are used by organized crime, some are used for clubs, some are used because of one's profession like the "Engineer's ring" which is worn because of a religious oath and promise to wear it on the little finger by all professional engineers who belong to Canadian and American engineer cults. Others will get a "class ring" for their school or get awarded a ring for winning a particular sports game. All these nonsensical rings (wastes of metal) have "special meaning" to their wearers because of the ancient magical history behind rings that has bled into our culture and remains to influence the behavior of many who don't know why the rings hold such importance in their lives. Most people don't have a valid reason to wear a piece of metal around their fingers, wrists, necks, ankles, ears, etc and are subconsciously doing so for religious reasons with a religious zeal which is wrong and wasteful for them to be doing. Prior to the pagan "oath ring" phenomenon when giving oaths people would make promises to someone while putting their hand under the person's left thigh. Biblically this is reported as being done when people made a promise to Abraham in Genesis 24:2, and to Israel/Jacob in Genesis 47:29. Anyways modern wedding rings are essentially a form of pagan "oath rings" which were a way of swearing in the name of other than God, which is a type of shirk(type of disbelief) which all prophets prohibited. Just consider how not a single prophet wore a wedding ring, and some of the prophets even had multiple wives yet wore no wedding rings and neither did their wives. The pagans did it because of magical reasons and based on their pagan doctrines. Thus today "wedding rings" should not be worn since they are a pagan prop for magic. In the Renaissance people were told Jewels were medicinal and if you ate a Jewel it cured bodily ailments, so people actually paid for expensive Jewels and ate them thinking they were medicine. Clearly rings still have a religious significance because nobody would pay the price if they didn't. To learn how religious people are about their rings you can ask someone in front of their spouse how much they are willing to sell their wedding ring to you for and see how they respond. So when people say their rings have no religious significance you can easily prove they are lying when you ask them to take their rings off and give them to you and never wear a ring again. Despite their love for money people still won't take off or stop wearing their magical wedding rings. Honestly most would not even stop in exchange for a monthly stipend because they actually have a magical belief about their rings even if they don't use the word magic. The prophets taught people how to get engaged and married the right way, but most people today are getting married the pagan magical way and then they wonder why they got so many problems. Then they buy rings or jewelry thinking that will fix it all or "ensure love", just as the pagans did except they got magic rings while today people get extravagant expensive diamond versions of magic rings without even intending them to be magical. Thus today many people are making it more expensive to perform pagan magical rituals and they do them not even knowing of the pagan magical origins. So they are actually worse than the pagans, because they do the same stuff without the foolish theological reasons and pay more today to do the ancient pagan love magic. It's simple if you want a happy successful marriage one follows the prophetic instructions, as with everything, not popular expensive nonsensical pagan magical familial superstitious customs. As the story about Adam and Eve getting tricked by Satan in the form of a snake goes, still many men and women get married in a way that is based on pagan magical snake religious rituals. Satan tricked Adam and Eve to do stupid things so they could stay in paradise in marital bliss forever and Satan tricks many humans to get married in sinful manners and do sinful stupid things in the hopes of eternal love/marital bliss. Always remember Satan can mess up a marriage even if the spouses continue to stay together forever, just being together does not mean it's a success. How can you tell if your marriage is a success? If you or both spouses are happy? Of course not! A marriage is only successful if it makes our Creator happy. Sorry for digressing from the topic to delve on weddings/rings but that is just one example of a pagan tradition that continues without knowledge of its pagan roots. So when you have such a glaring example of magical rites practiced by the masses til this day then do you not logically conclude that the creed of pagans has continued til this day as well without knowledge of its roots?

    Continuing with the snake cults, due to a lack of scientific knowledge pagans thought that snakes were both male and female. To reproduce it was believed that snakes would put their tale into their mouth and have their male tale ejaculate sperm into their female mouth which would impregnate themselves. The pagans also believed this was how dragons got pregnant as well. While for those who believed snakes were immortal magical creatures they started to believe self-sacrifice was required for eternal life, the sacrifice being that to gain their next day of life they had to eat their body or their bodily fluids in this day's life. As a result some crazy pagans would perform autofellatio and "eat their life force" so as to gain eternal life, since if their sexual liquid could give new life when put in the womb they thought it was some type of elixir. Others were not that flexible so those guys would just have women perform oral sex thinking it would make their women live forever. Of course some of these guys were smart enough to know it would not make the females live forever if they swallowed their seed but they figured it was a "white lie" they could live with telling under the circumstances and these scoundrels didn't really feel it was wrong to lie to get sexual pleasure. Little has changed, except the females who do such demeaning sexual activities to/for males today expect to get even less reward for it than the pagan females did. For some it was a serious religious sexual act that led to further male control over society as the female was deemed in need of male seed for survival. But what about the guys? How were they supposed to live forever, if they didn't want to consume male seed? Well for those who didn't try sodomy or homosexuality there was cannabalism, but few people adopted cannabalism because it was not practical, it led to social mistrust and to many it just didn't seem right especially since it didn't work for animals. Later this dilemma and religious stupidity is what led to the infamous mutual oral sex position named after a number which I'm not going to name because it's an abominable sin you shouldn't even know about to begin with, and I'm not teaching such evil. I learned about it in public school. But the position was practiced by Hindus and pagan Romans as part of their religions thousands of years ago. It only became popular in the West since 1912 CE when the magician Aleister Crowley wrote about it in a magic book of his saying it was *"The way to Succeed and Suck Eggs"*. By "Succeed" he sarcastically meant "Suck the male seed" and this act was part of a magical ritual. Whereas this is what makes immoral unnatural sex today so much worse, because the sexual positions people are doing have been the religious rituals of false religions for thousands of years but modern people just think it's creative enjoyable sex. Your religion determines how you have sex even down to the actual positions experienced. That's called practicing religion, it's not "just sex". Most people who have sex today are doing it in polytheistic ways according to many different religions and don't even know that the things they are doing are considered religious rituals and sometimes even magical rituals depending on the sex itself. So sex isn't something to play around with, it is a serious activity central to every religion. It is literally how humans reproduce themselves. Now do you really think that religions are not going to tell you exactly how to reproduce? Religions tell you how to do everything in life, do you think the actions during sexual reproduction and the continuation of life wouldn't have instructions too? This is why people in the past would only marry those who shared their faith, because people who have different religions have sex differently according to their belief and their particular religion's instructions. There is no such thing as "secular sex". In case you didn't know God has rules for spouses having sex, but don't get the wrong idea. When God tells one how to have sex, he knows what humans like better than we do. Nobody can tell God that they can give better instructions for sex, God knows our bodies. God knows best how when and with whom our sexual parts should fit together. Consider again if pagan sexual rituals are still practiced today without attribution to their origin then how foolish must it be to think the major pagan creeds just altogether vanished without a trace when people embraced Christianity?

Not all pagans believed that snakes reproduced by self-impregnating themselves or used that belief to facilitate unnatural sexual exploits. Some pagans considered snakes to be immortal and that they didn't reproduce at all but ate themselves because of the sacred Ouroborus, in their view, symbolized by the snake/dragon eating itself and not impregnating itself. Now you might be thinking that's not true and they couldn't have been that stupid to think snakes live forever by eating themselves. But even the famous philosopher Plato explained this as he is recorded to have written on snakes and the meaning behind the Ouroborus symbol as he personally interpreted it: "*The living being had no need of eyes because there was nothing outside of him to be seen; nor of ears because there was nothing to be heard; and there was no surrounding atmosphere to be breathed; nor would there have been any use of organs by the help of which he might receive his food or get rid of what he had already digested, since there was nothing which went from him or came into him: for there was nothing beside him. Of design he created thus; **his own waste providing his own food**, and all that he did or suffered taking place in and by himself. For the Creator conceived that a being which was self-sufficient would be far more excellent than one which lacked anything; and, as he had no need to take anything or defend himself against any one, the Creator did not think it* *necessary to bestow upon him hands: nor had he any need of feet, nor of the whole apparatus of walking; but the movement suited to his spherical form which was designed by him, being of all the seven that which is most appropriate to mind and intelligence; and he was made to move in the same manner and on the same spot, within his own limits revolving in a circle. All the other six motions were taken away from him, and he was made not to partake of their deviations. And as this circular movement required no feet, the universe was created without legs and without feet."*

I'm not saying Plato himself believed snakes survived by eating their own waste, but he believed this is what the Ouroborus symbolized a snake doing. Other pagans thought the same and figured all snakes lived that way and lived forever by eating themselves/their tail/their waste because snakes actually do bite their tails sometimes. Even today you can see snakes who bite their own tails and sometimes appear to be eating themselves. Eventually snake cults proliferated and snake worship became a popular type of religion. Of course any rational person would wonder how pagans could think snakes were immortal because of eating themselves when they must have seen dead snakes after they killed them in self-defense, or seen snakes eat other animals. Well this dilemma was explained by pagans saying that dead snakes would be resurrected from the dead and them eating other animals was their form of spiritual battle with other spiritual beings. Of course the Jewish story of Moses having his snake devour the other snakes further supported this pagan view that snakes would eat other animals as a method of warfare, not for nutrition. But what about snake immortality, how did they explain that one in the light of snake corpses? Well that's easy, obviously the snakes would be resurrected from the dead. Pagans had many theories how this happened which led to the infamous "Join or die" snake cartoon to motivate the American colonies to join together based on the superstition that if snake parts were joined together before sunset then they'd come back to life again but few of these theories had strong evidence aside from popularity. To pagans popularity was a proof, if it was popularly believed that meant it was proven. If the popularity proof wasn't enough for some then pagans would simply retort "It's a mystery." it didn't have to make sense or be proven for them to believe it. It was just a sacred mystery that they believed was true and held the key for eternal life, thus it became a central tenet in some snake worshipping cults. If there were any who ever doubted the resurrection of snakes, then there would always be some fool who said that they saw with their own eyes a dead snake, and days later they saw the same exact snake alive moving about in a different place as if it had never been dead. Sometimes many would witness some snake who had died and been "resurrected, so people believed it to be true thinking they wouldn't lie about such a thing, I mean they were literally eye witnesses, it wasn't some book they had read, they actually saw this stuff with their own eyeballs. How could anyone argue with that? Some could even bring you to the snake or bring it to you and show you it really is alive and pagan priests would allege to have the same snakes in their temples for centuries ever-living. The pagans didn't lie about seeing the snakes, the snakes just looked so similar that they thought it was the same snake and assumed it was resurrected from the dead or immortal instead of realizing it was a different but similar looking snake. It's sounds funny but it's sad because this was their religion. Today some Christians will tell you that their leaders turn bread and wine into Jesus' body and blood, literally every Sunday despite it still being the same according to all human senses. Snakes were naturally considered intelligent, since they were immortal, and they could be inhabited by the gods or goddesses. Many myths existed of gods taking a snake form to interact with humans on earth, since they couldn't well interact in their god or goddess form. Sometimes such transfigurations even involved births. For example Olympias the wife of Phillip of Macedon belonged to the orgiastic cult of Dionysius and she would sleep with snakes. Phillip didn't really like her too much and wasn't too keen on having sex with her either, I mean afterall she would keep snakes in her bed some of which were poisonous, today we'd say that's a crazy lady. Once while Phillip was off waging war legend has it that Zeus turned into a snake to have sex with Olympias and before Phillip returned she gave birth to her son named Alexander, who historians call Alexander the Great.   Thus Alexander was the son of Zeus who impregnated his mother while Zeus was in snake form. In China they believed a snake God with the head of a woman, called Nuwa, was the creator of humans. Greeks thought the snake Ophion had incubated a big egg from which everything in the world hatched. Egyptians believed in the snake god Amduat who existed before everything else and was the ancestor of the god Ra and the Sun. Amduat allegedly would die every night and be reborn every morning yet there were many snake deities of Egypt such as Meretseger, Nehebkau, Renenutet and Wadjet. Egyptians revered snake deities so much, the Pharaohs would even wear a cobra effigy on their crown. Whereas this is why the miracle of Moses and his staff turning into a snake has so many lessons in it. When the magicians made their ropes seem to be snakes, the people basically thought they were witnessing their many gods slithering around this Moses guy who claimed his God was the only real god. What could Moses do with such "proof" to the contrary when they could visibly see their many gods in snake form? Well it is known what Moses did when he threw down his staff and it became a snake that swallowed up all the magicians false works/false gods. While although texts describe the magicians as magicians in historical context that wasn't the only thing they were. In the ancient past, the magicians were the priests of the pagans and their doctors. They were similar to Native American Shamans who were both healers and "holy men" that were considered as such because of their magic. So Moses actually defeated Priestly Doctors who used magic and this is why many of the subsequent plagues involved medical afflictions or economic destruction, because the magicians were the doctors and as priests they would do the fertility rituals as well as the rituals for the Nile river. Thus all the plagues the Egyptians were later afflicted with were all things the magicians were supposed to be preventing as part of their job. But they sensibly quit and joined Moses' team when they saw his miracle, unfortunately this may have caused the Egyptians to incorrectly think their calamities were simply because the magician priest doctors quit their jobs. After his victory Moses picked up the conquering snake and held it as his staff once more. This wasn't the first time that Moses had picked up a snake and had it turn into a staff and Pharaoh knew what that meant. A snake was the prime symbol on Pharaoh's crown, so with Moses picking up the snake and having it become his staff Pharaoh knew this meant Moses was the one who is supposed to have the political authority and rulership in the land. Snakes were dangerous to just pick them up by the tail, you needed authority to do it safely. Thus when magicians did their magic they did it in the name of Pharaoh because the religious belief dictated he had religious and political authority and if the magicians were to try to pick up their snakes they would've also done it in the name of Pharaoh, which they would've had to do because they already knew Moses had done his staff-snake-staff miracle before. They were told Moses was just a magician and planned to fight his magic with their own and then pick up their fake snakes in Pharaoh's name showing Pharaoh was in the right. When the masses then saw Moses' miracle they knew it was both a declaration and proof of religious and political authority over all, especially since he didn't cast or pick up his snake in Pharaoh's name but in the name of God instead. Politically speaking Moses was divinely appointed as leader in front of everybody and he simultaneously was divinely proven to be the prophet of the people at the same time he proved their false deities were not deities at all. This one miracle basically exposed and refuted everything about the whole wicked religious and political Egyptian system and everyone saw it. Yet Pharaoh did not accept this religious or political statement. However that wasn't all Moses did to make his case, since most people accused him of sorcery after his miracles God gave him a miracle to refute that claim too. Moses would put his left hand under his shirt and then bring it forth and it shined with a whiteness brighter than the sun. This sign was important for multiple reasons. 1. It refuted any who worshipped the sun and belonged to sun cults because visibly the left hand of Moses was brighter and gave better guidance than the very sun pagans were worshipping. 2. Black magic was called the "left hand path" and white magic was called the "right hand path" yet the shining white hand of Moses was his left hand. So it couldn't have been white magic because it would've been the right hand and it couldn't be black magic because it was white light, thus this sign violated the very principles of black magic and white magic so it could not possibly be any type of magic. It was also another political statement because Pharaohs were thought to be descendants of the sun/sun deities. Although Moses was giving off a brighter light than Pharaoh ever did or could, once more showing that Pharaoh was in the darkness of ignorance, arrogance and disbelief. Thereby implying with a sign as bright as the sun that Pharaoh was not fit to be followed religiously nor politically and that all the popular mainstream ancient religious Egyptian cultural faiths were false and Moses had the exclusive religion of truth.

The Greeks used a snake symbol too but called it the "Rod of Asclepius".

Despite the Greek Hippocrates being credited as the founder of medicine, when it came to medicine the Greeks were quite dumb. The ancient Greeks intertwined medicine with their pagan religions. For most ailments they had absolutely no remedy at all, and knew practically nothing about the female body thinking menses was failed sperm and that the womb wandered around inside the body. To be a doctor of Greek medicine meant you were a pagan priest too since the gods played the key role in Greek medicine. Aside from a few herbal remedies most Greek "medicine" consisted of folk healers using amulets, charms and spells. Asclepius was the god of healing and in Greece if you were sick or in need of a cure for some injury or disability you had to go to the temple of Asclepius in the city of Epidarus. What if one couldn't travel to the temple? Well then such person would just have to live as they were or try buying some special charms if they were desperate.

For the few who were able to travel to the city of Epidarus and visit the temple of Asclepius they'd go to an Asclepiede who was part priest and part physician. You see as the god of healing all things medicinal it was henceforth pagan theology that if you weren't a priest of the god of healing you didn't know much at all about healing, unless you had military experience. But how did Asclepius become the god of healing? Well according to the greeks the god Apollo had sex with a girl named Coronis and she got pregnant. However this girl apparently was a busy lady and had sex with other beings as well so Apollo got mad that she cheated on him and killed her. Yet as she was laid on her funeral pyre to be cremated, the baby in her womb was taken out by Apollo and allegedly he was still alive and named Asclepius. One day Asclepius did something nice to a snake so the snake licked his ears clean and in doing so imparted the secret knowledge to him. This was possibly because Greeks revered snakes thinking they were sacred endowed with immortality, healing and wisdom. Asceplius would then have a snake on his rod or wand which he used to go around and heal people with whenever they were sick or anything was wrong. Some actually called it a wand and the symbol is also known as the "Wand of Asclepius" as well, because he was basically a magician. Asclepius was such a healer he apparently didn't let people die and would bring people back to life from the dead, making death into just another type of sickness that would be cured by the rod/wand of Asclepius. But since nobody was dying anymore the population allegedly got out of control so much to such an absurd extent that Zeus had to kill Asclepius so people would die again without him bringing them back to life. Asclepius was killed by Zeus because he was giving everyone eternal life via his snake rod/wand and earth couldn't sustain such a large eternal population, and Hades was getting upset that nobody else was coming to the Underworld and Asceplius had taken everyone out of the Underworld by resurrecting all the dead with his snake rod/wand. Yet what really ticked off Zeus was that Asclepius got paid in gold for bringing Hippolytus back to life. Thus Zeus killed Asclepius with a thunderbolt. But this made Apollo upset, so Apollo killed the Cyclopes who made Zeus's thunderbolts. In response to that Zeus removed Apollo from the night sky for a year forcing him to serve the King of Thessaly. After that Zeus brought Apollo back to the sky and resurrected his Cyclopses; he'd have thunderbolts once more while Apollo would be in the night sky. To end the feud the body of Asclepius was made into the constellation Ophiuchus, which is the same constellation as Serpetarius which is known as the "Serpent-Bearer" constellation depicted as a man grasping the serpent constellation of Serpetus. Clearly this pagan myth has biblical themes of a snake giving knowledge that results in eternal life but the story continues. Asclepius had sex with Epione who was the goddess of the soothing of pain. Of the 8 children Asclepius had the girls were goddesses like their mother and the guys were humans like their father.

Two notable daughters of Asclepius stand out, Panacea the goddess of medicines and Hygieia the goddess of hygiene. Hygieia was more about preventing sickness than curing it. Her symbol was the "Bowl of Hygieia".

    The snake of the "Bowl of Hygieia" is thought to play a similar role as the snake in the rod/wand of Asclepius except it also has a human symbolism. The human personification of the snake was that each person must decide on whether they want the hygiene of hygieia. If so and they then choose to drink of her cup they'll have eternal life. But hygiene isn't always fun so not everyone will choose it. This is in contrast to Asclepius's rod which would give people eternal life without their consent. Asclepius saw it as a duty to stop and cure death, Hygieia offered eternal life with conditions and rather than give it to all she just made a offer, but if you didn't accept it then you would die. This "Bowl of Hygieia" is thought to have also been the original "Holy Grail" that would literally provide eternal life if you drank from it's cup. But for those/all who couldn't find the real cup they could go to a temple of Hygieia and drink from the cups offered by the pagan priests of the cult of Hygieia in order to get eternal life. You see the pagan priests taught you didn't really need to drink from the literal cup of Hygieia or the actual liquid that she served, you could just drink from one her priests temple cups drinking the temple liquid and it would be exactly the same as if you drank it from Hygieia's sacred swill directly. Obviously it sounds a lot like the Christian communion ceremony and Christian doctrines about salvation. But this was what Greeks taught and believed centuries before Jesus was born and BEFORE Paul came to preach to them. But the symbolism and commonalities with Christianity doesn't stop there. There is the "Crucified Serpent" or Alchemy cross which was the symbol of Alchemy and the miraculous "elixir of Mercury" which was thought to provide great health benefits for many centuries.

Snakes also shed their skin which influenced ideas of reincarnation or rebirth but for pagans there was a mystery of how/why snakes shed their skins. Was it a part of them being resurrected from the dead? Or was it something else? Surely it couldn't be so simple as them just growing and scratching it off, there had to be some special sacred mystery to it. Some pagans witnessed snakes going into water, of which water was essential to life for all things but not snakes since they were immortal and logically one would think snakes would hate water and that it'd be dangerous since they would get completely submerged and likely drown. Therefore snakes must surely have been going into water for some reason that was necessary for their eternal lives. The pagans figured the snake must go into the water purposely so it's skin gets wet, afterwhich it emerges sheds it's skin and then is reborn in a sense with all the dirt that it had accumulated throughout it's life being removed as it's skin was removed. A similar process happens with human births when the water breaks and then the baby emerges with an umbilical cord attached, symbolizing a snake, which must be shed/cut for the human child's future life. The water breaking was a mystery of birth, since the mother hadn't drank that much water the womb water was considered special. Some pagans even speculated that the womb water was originally sperm and that men were nearly 100% responsible for the formation of the baby in that their physical part would shape/form the baby when it was inside the uterus and then the sperm deposited would become the womb water. Hence it was thought that without the sperm "making the womb water" no baby could be formed/born since the "sacred water" was needed for birth/life. The blessed birth water of the womb was possibly a sign in human births so pagans would learn the snakes submerge themselves in water deliberately to emerge reborn, but before they can truly experience eternal life their snake skin must be violently shed and removed. Thus that explained the mystery. Logically if snakes just did the violent scratching without their ritual water submersion then the dirt wouldn't fully get cleaned and the dirt on their skins would get on their new skins carrying over with them into their future life. Therefore for the violent sacrifice of their snake form to count and get them a fresh clean slate or skin they needed the water ritual and it was all thought of as a sign of the gods/goddesses some of whom became snakes once in awhile so that humans would learn the secret to the snake's eternal life. Yet this water ritual and violent shedding of skin, and sometimes blood if the snake was rough, was not enough because there was the Ouroborus and the snake eating itself for eternal life, or impregnating itself if you held one of those types of pagan snake beliefs. Thus there was the water, the shedding of the body(and sometimes blood) and the eating of itself for eternal life. The gods/goddesses also were even documented to have become snakes every so often to teach humans the mystery of immortality and eternal life. Some humans even speculated that it was possible for a human to become a snake and thus live forever. There were other animals believed to resurrect themselves too such as the Phoenix but we cannot possibly list all the pagan beliefs in detail in one book. Nevertheless along came Saul/Paul, the name changer and the game changer who changed the name/game of religions forever.

    Remember the pagans thought snakes were knowledgeable of divine wisdom, so when you have that type of religious belief everybody seems smart. So when Paul came and taught all the pagans that Jesus gave his body and blood in sacrifice and ate his own body and blood in the form of bread and wine so that all can attain eternal life if they accept him as god and eat him in bread and blood form, he was preaching to the choir. Jesus in the pagan eyes was the snake of the rod/wand of Ascelpius and the snake of Ouroborus combined with the choice of the Bowl of Hygieia. With the "Crucified Serpent" and "Seal of Caligostro" easily becoming the doctrine of the Atonement for Original sins and all other sins of mankind via the cross they were told Jesus died on. Plus the baptism ritual was the same as the fertility myths and already had been practiced by trinitarian cults for centuries. Paul didn't really teach pagans anything at all like a new religion he just upgraded their religion and expanded upon it, quite masterfully. He syncretised the pagan snake cults into Christianity, and they loved it because handling snakes was kind of dangerous anyways. This fusion was aided by the fact that snake cults were only one type of pagan religion. Thereby obfuscation aided the blending mix when the solar cults, vegetation cults, saviour cults and mystery religions each added their own impression upon the composite Paulian faith. Once these groups merged, the ingredients to the recipe became less identifiable and then a Jewish splinter sect made everything worse. These were the Jewish magicians known as Kabbalists. Saul/Paul may have been one of them or he might not have been, I don't have evidence to label him as one or not. However the symbols of Kabbalism made their mark on Christian iconography and the snake cultists loved their symbols. One such ancient Kabbalistic magic symbol was the "tree of life" with a snake being the main attraction of the depiction. Which doesn't really look like a tree at all but more of a cross.

To increase it's potency as a magical symbol, the Ouroborus was frequently made in knotted form such as this.

Personally I feel the knot Ouroborus looks like a cross which is in a very familiar style that is used in Christian crosses to this day, without the snake features. However the point worth making is that crosses and snakes went together in both magical faiths and snake cults. Many pagans would have no issue with a cross symbol with a self-sacrificial being that symbolized eternal life. Most pagans already had, used and adored such symbols. Artifacts exist which prove that the cross was a popular pagan image. Many pagans adored crosses prior to Christianity ever existing.

The Ouroborus is also part of the religion of Kundalini Yoga, but the bit I find most interesting is the Ouroborus of Hinduism. In Hinduism instead of halos, their deities are commonly found with Ouroboruses. Carl Jung explained about the Hindu Ouroborus that: "*Shakti is represented as a snake wound three and a half times round the lingam, which is Shiva in the form of a phallus.*" Shiva is the goddess of creation and destruction and thus the Ouroborus around her represents the creative destruction of life and death key to the Hindu belief about reincarnation. That Jung described Shiva as the "form of a phallus" is very telling, because the phalluses were integral to the solar cults and the pagan sons of god cults. Another meaning of the Ouroborus symbol is that it represents the cycle of life and infinity because at the beginning when the serpent or a dragon eats its tails, it means there is a chaos while at the middle of a serpent it can represent a peace, but at the end where the tail is bitten it symbolizes the chaos again and this process continues forever. What's the point? Well Wolf-Dieter Storl stated "*When Shakti is united with Shiva, she is a radiant, gentle goddess; but when she is separated from him, she turns into a terrible, destructive fury. She is the endless Ouroboros, the dragon biting its own tail, symbolizing the cycle of samsara.*" How is Christianity different? Christians say the Old Testament God was vengeful and full of wrath until he was united and became all-merciful once Jesus came on the scene. While Jesus is said to be the word in the beginning, then the word made flesh to be crucified in the middle for the Original sins and everyone's sins, who will come again at the end in the times of chaos to restore the balance thus ensuring eternal life based on "following the words of the Word of God (the bible) which says to follow the "Word of God" (Jesus) who is the "Word made flesh"". It's a tri-word trinity all taught in a language Jesus never spoke. That's the Christian narrative in that the Word in the beginning turns into flesh and since the paper Word says this it must be true and thus the Christian says the words they say thinking it's what the Word of God (don't ask me which) taught/teaches/wants. Oh and in case you didn't know they say that "the Word" is eternal without beginning or end and that "the Word made flesh" sacrificed itself so "the Word" would survive. With poetic justice the Greek word the Christians use for "the Word" when referring to the Word in the beginning, the Word in the flesh, Jesus in the middle, and Jesus or God in the end is "Logos" the same exact word pagans used for their trinitarian deities. Their doctrine of "the Word" is nearly identical to the false pagan doctrines taught by the Ouroborus logos. So Christians do indeed follow the logos, but it's the pagan logos that they copied and altered into their own while copying the pagan titles, rituals and mottos deciding to kill, condemn or ignore anyone who objects or exposes them. Also Jung labeled Shiva as the form of the phallus when the Shakti Ouroborus is wound around her. So we get a picture of the Ouroborus around a Phallus. While phallus idols represented penis or the "*Sun of God*". To the snake cults the snake was it's own tool of sacrifice as well as the one being sacrificed. So it really was a tough mix to combine their two prime symbols. Although a snake and a penis could in theory work, those types of pagans were not the most influential in the art department of the Christian faith. The saviour sons of gods, trinitarian and mystery faiths were accustomed to cross symbols with and without their object of worship on it. So there was heavy pressure to keep the symbol of a man on a cross from those pagans and the solar cults would be satisfied as long as the phrase "son of God" were around and a man on a cross was much more artistic than a obelisk statue of a penis, with the snake cult already employing crosses in their own faiths. But how to make such a combo pagan symbol and relate it somehow to Jesus? Well that's where the pagans decided to adopt the anti-snake Jewish history and the new doctrine of mankind's Original Sin helped them greatly. Since snakes were the bad guys in Jewish customs due to the fall of humans resulting from their interaction with Satan in the form of a snake according to the bible, if Jesus was to be a sacrifice for eternal life the snake could be incorporated into the new Christian logo without having any snakes visible by saying the act of Jesus dying on a cross defeated the chaos caused by the snake in the beginning. In plain terms the symbol of Jesus on a cross was given the meaning of being a redemption for the "Original Sin" which humans got because of a snake near the beginning of everything. Thus if Satan was the snake and Jesus achieved a total victory over Satan for eternal life then there is the first part of the Ouroborus interwoven with the new symbol. But what about the end of the Ouroborus? The Ouroborus snake doctrine had an end to it as well. How to include the Ouroborus in the end? Simple. Even though the sacrifice supposedly defeats Satan the snake in the middle of the timeline, since the snake was at the beginning and Jesus was also sharing part of the eternal snake myth then Jesus was said to exist at the beginning too. Yet the bad snake Satan must exist at the end so that's where the apocolyptic biblical stories of Satan the "accursed serpent" and/or the red dragon were included in Christian doctrines. Whereas Jesus since he had in reality promised to come back near the end of the world, then Christians had his story changed to say he will slay the snake/dragon/satan near the chaotic period around the end of time instead of a specific human who claimed to be divine as Jesus originally promised to do. Thus the snake cults got almost all of their eternal self-sacrificing snake myths to split into Jesus in some respects and Satan in other respects, with both having existed at the beginning of the world and at the end, with the sacrifice and the violent chaos at the end of time. But what about the chaos at the beginning of time? The Original Sin story accounted for the victory of snake like Jesus defeating the snake plan of snake Satan thus giving snake cultists a eternal life outcome via snake eat snake sacrifice, but the snake chaos had to exist at the beginning of the story. The Original Sin story didn't have the chaos the snake cultists needed. Since Satan was the bad snake and villain of the tale he had to be charged with chaos. Yet if he wasn't divine or a son of God he could not have a part to play in the beginning, especially with chaos because power was needed to cause chaos. So to satisfy the snake cultists Satan had to become powerful, yet the doctrine wouldn't allow for a evil snake Satan created powerful because that just didn't fit with the lying snake Original Sin story. What was powerful that existed in the beginning that wasn't God or Jesus? Angels. Therefore Satan was labeled as an angel turned evil, surely such a change would cause lots of chaos. To make the story interesting the good angels were said to have waged war with Satan's angels thereby making angel fight angel perfectly imitating the snake/dragon eating itself at the beginning since the same species fought each other. For extra measure the good angels would again fight the bad angels at the chaotic end thus fully completing the snake cultist circle of life. Yet the question Christians never ask is that *"If angels fought Satan the alleged angel and his alleged army of fallen angels since before man existed then why haven't they been able to kill Satan yet? Or have they stopped fighting? Why doesn't God kill Satan if he is a fallen angel instead of killing himself or son in the form of Jesus?"* It's because Satan is not a angel and serves a purpose to God by existing and his plots only harm the disobedient ungrateful. It's because the fallen angel story is a slanderous myth that those questions are never asked or answered. Myths are never analyzed critically. After these mythical additions the snake cultists thereby had the entire Ouroborus myth included in Christianity and could justify their concession of not using snake imagery in the prominent Christian symbols of salvation. Each pagan group had to give up something, so in order for the snake cultists to give up their popular snake imagery they got their whole Ouroborus doctrine included as part of the faith, just cloaked in different vocabulary. Each pagan philosophy contributed their own doctrines, some more than others and some were shared by many types. When one makes the connection that Jesus is replaced with the pagan phallus idols and combine that with the eternal life giving rod of Ascelpius, the Christian story of the snake causing Original Sin with the Christian's subsequent doctrine of the crucifiction of Jesus rectifying that Serpentine effect one realizes its the same old myth using Jesus as the main character and the cross as the relic that gets it's powers from or conquers the power/poison of the snake. However if this age-old religion of initial chaos being fixed by some son of god savior who grants eternal life to everybody, whether he's called Asclepius or Jesus, only to return to chaos once more until the savior deity reestablishes the power of their self-sacrifice then the prophets of God must have known and been exposed to this. Afterall it's proven the Ouroborus, and the rod of Asceplius and this stuff existed during the times of biblical prophets. Did they have anything to do with this? Well there was Moses. He was given a special sign where he'd throw down a stick, and it'd turn into a snake and then when he picked it up it'd turn back into a stick. Is that a myth too? No this was a refutation of snake myths. The pagans believed in this circular snake scam religion thinking theirs was the original faith and that Moses wasn't in the right. Thus this sign of Moses and his stick-snake-stick displayed that their whole religion of the Ouroborus was a false premise. The first snake had to be created prior to eating anything, even if it survived by eating itself. Who created everything before the beginning? The one who made Moses a prophet and turned his stick into a snake. Then does universal existence keep going on forever? No it will end and the living creatures, like snakes and humans will be brought back to the one who sent them to earth and created them to begin with. This sign proved the pagan religions false and established that eternal life was only to be attained through the religion of Moses. Yet it didn't stop there, there was the famous test of Moses vs. the magicians. That battle ended with Moses' stick turning into a snake which did not eat itself, as falsehood is bound to do, but it ate the falsehood and returned to Moses as a stick once more. This is what happens in life. God sends the truth, and it destroys the falsehood. There is no eternal circle where a noble self-sacrificing being saves everyone for eternity due to the actions of an abusive parent god. Life is a test for all to do what they were given life to do before they are recalled, to be punished or rewarded. The snake was created out of a stick by God to do a job, it did it's job, it returned to being a stick, then God turned it into a snake again to do a job which it did and then it returned to it's non-existent state. The stick/snake had no choice in the matter of it's life or non-life, it existed through no willpower of it's own and couldn't travel between states of existence but was put when and where it's life giver deemed. The one who gave life temporarily to Moses' staff is the same one which gave us life to do a job and will cause us to die, give us life again and reward or punish according to our job performance throughout our life.

Many Christians reading this might say the snake cults and other pagan faiths were all part of God's plan to guide the pagans to Christianity and the bible. But we must remember the bible did not exist until hundreds of years after Jesus, it was not written until AFTER Paul started preaching to these snake cults. Thus if one is writing a book for people with such snake/sun/saviour beliefs to get them to change to your faith then it's easy to make up such details so it seems like the snake cults foreshadowed the biblical stories. In reality the bible authors just wrote those details to make their target audience think it was the answer/final explanation to their mysteries. But most importantly the beliefs of the snake worshippers were wrong. Snakes and dragons don't eat themselves, get reborn, reincarnate, get resurrected or impregnate themselves. So if one wants to say their prior beliefs led them to embrace Christianity when has falsehood ever prepared people for the prophetic truth? Name one prophet where the polytheistic people upon falsehood when they heard of what a prophet of God taught said "*Oh yeah that's just like our religion, but our religion is totally wrong and this is totally right from God almighty.*" Is that what people said to Noah, Abraham, Moses or even Jesus? Because one must remember Jesus was around and knew of these snake cults and the snake worshippers. So if these pagans were getting prepared for Christianity why didn't he tell anybody and why doesn't the world of Christendom tell people? Really if God wanted these pagans to have such beliefs to facilitate their conversion to Christianity then why hasn't this been preached publicly by the Christian world? Why do they hide this information about the pagan religions? Because the whole "*pagans believed in Christianity before Jesus came because Christianity is true and God was preparing them for the truth*" is just a desperate excuse for Christians who have no other explanation to justify their personal faith in Christianity once they discover the pagans already believed in the very doctrines which they hear in church and read in their bibles. Some might wonder why the pagans never had a popular religious text. But who ever said the bible wasn't the pagan world's religious book? There was just one big problem with the snake cults converting to Christianity and that is the people who truly followed Jesus knew about the snake cults and knew they were upon falsehood. They also had very different ideas and attitudes about snakes than the snake cultists did. So how then did the snake cult members blend their idea of Jesus being the sacred snake with the Jewish history of anti-snake doctrines? Via violence.

    Undoubtedly Saul/Paul had access to and inspiration from ancient pagan beliefs when formulating his doctrine. Paul's teachings were nearly a carbon copy of combined pagan religions, with the only difference being the name of the "crucified savior/ divine son". The idea of a divine son of God who was part of a trinity being crucified for the sins of mankind was already a common belief held throughout the pagan roman empire. The Jews witnessed this and would have known not to believe in anything like it. When qualities of one set of beliefs are absorbed under another religious code it is called Syncretism, and this is not how the religion of the prophets developed. Prophets received inspiration, syncretism is how man-made religions developed. Owing to the syncretism of the Pauline doctrine it is unlikely he was inspired as he claimed to be. Many pagans were already doing what Saul/Paul would later say were divinely inspired rituals taught exclusively to him by God and/or Jesus. It actually seems that the pagans taught Paul instead of Paul teaching the pagans. Afterall it is easier to take something from another religion and absorb it into your own rather than having people give it up, this strategy makes it much easier to gain converts. That's not how the prophets worked, but it does seem like that was Saul/Paul's method of operating. Not everyone believed Saul/Paul was genuine, nor did they accept his new doctrine because they had their own gospels, alleged to have been written by Thomas, James, Peter, Mary, Barnabas and many others. They taught a very different version of Jesus than the one preached by Paul; who never met Jesus while he was on earth. Although not all of these gospels were actually written by the one whom the texts claim, often they were written pseudonymously. Some were forgeries and others were changed after being written by the copiers, intentionally and unintentionally. Essentially every church had a different understanding of Jesus based on different scriptures and there was little uniformity among early Christians. This continued for some time with different denominations denouncing the others as heretics. Everyone was claiming to be followers of Jesus, frequently their arguments would turn violent and blood would be shed. This continued until Constantine became the emperor of Rome and wanted the chaos to stop in order to rule over a unified empire. Constantine called for the Council of Nicea in 325 CE inviting the leaders of different denominations to end the bickering and agree, hoping that one day Christianity could potentially unify the expansive Roman empire and be used as a political tool for control. Many bishops from all over the world with different theologies attended this council. The various bishops all brought their own scriptures with them in order to support their religious beliefs. Some bishops had all their expenses paid for by Constantine before they were "convinced" they should attend. Some church laws that were made official at the council of Nicaea include:

- The prohibition of usury among the clergy.

- The declaration of the invalidity of the baptism ritual done by Paulian heretics.

- The prohibition of kneeling on Sundays and during the Pentecost. (Standing was the normal posture for prayer at that time. Kneeling was for penitential prayer, not to be done at Sunday services which were of a festive nature in remembrance of Easter.)

- His declaration that the Roman Sun-day was to be the Christian Sabbath.

- He borrowed the emblem of the Sun-god (the cross of light) to be the emblem of Christianity.

- He adopted the traditional birthday of the Sun-god, and established the twenty-fifth of December, as the birthday of Jesus.

- He ordered for a statue of Jesus to replace the idol of the Sun-god, and decided to incorporate the ceremonies and rituals which were performed at the Sun-god's birthday celebrations into Christian ceremonies and rituals.

- He ruled that Christian clergymen shouldn't have intercourse with their wives after being ordained as priests. (At that time priests were still allowed to get married and have kids.)

These changes would make non-Christian pagans more comfortable on Christian holidays since all citizens would be celebrating the same way, on the same day, but just in different places using different phrases. The Roman Empire essentially became what we today call interfaith and the idea began to spread that everyone was all worshipping the same god, but just in different ways. The differences between religions were minimized to promote a common culture and it was difficult to tell who was worshipping Jesus, who was worshipping Mithras and who was worshipping Osiris because all the different places of worship were doing many things the same. This fusion of one or more gods combining to become one god is called theocrasia. It took a learned theologian to tell the difference between a pagan and a Christian. Sometimes today it still takes a theologian to tell the difference between a Christian and a non-Christian if the Christian isn't wearing a cross, even Christians have a hard time identifying fellow Christians.

Not everyone who called themselves followers of Jesus accepted these later to be adopted propositions. The bishop Arius denounced these aberrations and resisted, maintaining that Jesus was not equal to God nor the "son of God", but a miraculously created man who taught us to worship our Creator alone. It is said that after hearing this at the council of Nicaea the real "Saint" Nicholas went over to Arius and slapped/punched him in the face. As happens today the different religious denominations continuously bickered refusing to agree, with each sticking to their own scriptures as the only "true proof", or using their fists as proof as "Saint" Nicholas allegedly did. That's what usually happens when a religious person can't win a debate because what they believe is wrong but they refuse to lose and want the other party to change their religious opinion, they resort to violence. A pagan at the time, Constantine was no theologian, he was a politician who had no patience for further arguing. The bishops adjourned for the day and were ordered to leave all their gospels behind them in a big pile in the center of the room. The doors were locked and the bishops were told to pray that God would sort it all out. There were between 270-4,000 different gospels in there such as the Gospel of Phillip, the Gospel of Peter, the Gospel of Thomas, the Gospel of Judas, the Gospel of Truth, the Gospel of Mary, the Gospel of Mary Magdalene, the Gospel of the Nazarites and many others we don't know the titles of. When they opened the doors the next day, under the impression that no one had been inside since the day before, it was discovered that all but 4 books were thrown about and scattered across the room making it completely disorganized while the 4 gospels of Matthew, Mark, Luke and John were neatly placed on the long meeting table. The bishops were told it was a sign from God that no one could doubt, even though there were no witnesses and it is unknown who had the keys to the doors on that night. Irenaeus says there had to be exactly 4 gospels no more and no less, because there are 4 winds of the earth and 4 corners of the earth.(thus people thought the world was flat) Why did they think there were 4 corners of earth? Because in the bible Isaiah 11:12 says, *"He will set up a banner for the nations, And will assemble the outcasts of Israel, And gather together the dispersed of Judah From the four corners of the earth."* Likewise the verses of Job 38:13, Jeremiah 16:19, Daniel 4:11 and Isaiah 40:22 mentioning the "ends of the earth" and God sitting upon the "circle of the earth" was interpreted to mean that "the earth" is flat on the bottom with 4 corners but in the middle it has a half-dome shape giving it some vertical depth as though it were a 3-d object resting on a flat surface with the whole model being called earth instead of just the half-dome part. Anyways since the Old Testament taught the world had 4 corners then there were to be 4 gospels, no more no less. At that time instead of being called Sacred Scripture the 4 chosen books were called *"Memoirs of the apostles"*. Thereafter the 4 gospels of Matthew, Mark, Luke, and John became popular. Although these versions of Matthew, Mark, Luke and John are not the same as we have today, none of them were in English. They consisted of gospels written in Hebrew, Aramaic and Syriac with the oldest versions being written in Greek. It was ordered that all the other gospels, which people still considered authentic scriptures, were to be burned and banned throughout the Roman Empire and those found with such gospels were killed on the spot. Millions were killed. Thus many of these gospels have been lost to us forever, with only a few surviving the mass-burnings. People risked their lives hiding second hand copies of the originals of these banned gospels that were to be found by later generations. Many were rediscovered at Nag Hammadi. Some gospels have been excavated from graves like the Gospel of Barnabas found in Barnabas' grave in 478 CE. Although modern Christians claim Barnabas' grave had a gospel of Matthew in it, but that makes no sense. Think about it, why would Barnabas who wrote his own gospel which was later banned be buried with Matthew's gospel when Matthew's gospel was written after Barnabas had died? You can't get buried with a book that's not written yet! If not for such grave excavations we wouldn't have any information about the contents of these early Christian gospels aside from what heresiologists of the Trinitarian Church said they contained. Since these gospels have been rediscovered it has become evident that the early Church fathers didn't always tell the truth about what these other gospels said. Despite the ban, Arius continued teaching what he thought was the truth about Jesus, his motto was "*Follow Jesus as he preached*". Arius was branded heretical because his motto meant rejecting Paul and Trinitarianism. Those who believed as Arius did were persecuted in Northern Africa, the Middle East and Eastern Europe for many years but then the truth of their doctrine spread and Arius was made bishop of Constantinople. Interestingly arians didn't persecute the trinitarians where they were the majority but the trinitarians persecuted arians where arians were the minority. After Arius was murdered in 336 CE, the emperor Constantine reflected and recanted his previous religious beliefs becoming an Arian.(not to be confused with Aryan) Constantine then believed that the brand of Christianity he had previously helped to create and promote was a heresy and proclaimed that Paul was a false teacher, Constantine died the next year in 337 CE. The next emperor, Constantine's son Constantius II, was enthusiastically Arian and rejected the idea that Jesus was divine, even exiling the Trinitarian Roman Pope Liberius to Thrace. During the reign of Constantinus II it was commonly held that the Arian Unitarian Christian faith was true and that the Pauline Trinitarian belief was false, the majority of Christians in the Roman Empire were Arians believing that Jesus was a 100% human prophet sent by the One God who created everything. Things changed when Theodosius I became the roman emperor, he didn't believe in the doctrine promoted by Arius. Theodosius decreed the Pauline version of Christianity that was practiced in the city of Rome was to become the official religion of the Roman Empire in 380 CE. This was 18 years after the emperor Julian had proclaimed freedom of religion throughout the Roman Empire. Pauline Christianity ended religious freedom in the Roman Empire. It then became a crime to believe anything about Jesus that was different than the Trinitarian church of Rome, or to believe in any other religion; with the exception being Judaism. All other versions of Christianity that were not Roman Catholic were declared heretical, eventually made extinct through force. The law courts of Rome, called Basilicas, were turned into Catholic places of worship/preaching. Many people were killed because they didn't believe in what the church of Rome believed in. Ironically 30 years after the Roman Empire became Catholic, the Germanic Arians sacked Rome in 410, 455 and 546 CE destroying the Roman Empire. It's ironic because the early Catholic Church leaders preached that God would cause the Roman empire to prosper and expand since it had made what they considered "*the truth*" the official religion. To which non-Catholic Christians will say that Rome fell because they chose the wrong version of Christianity and not theirs, to which I say even if there is a right form of Christianity there is no right form of the bible because the corrupters were the compilers of the bible. It was not the case that the bible was made and then Christianity was corrupted as many Christians believe/hope, Christianity was corrupted the minute Jesus miraculously left Earth without dying and it is proven to have been corrupted hundreds of years before the first edition of the bible was compiled. Rather Rome declined as it unified upon greater error and downgraded from paganism to Christianity. The proliferation of sin leads wicked sinners to see the cross/christ as their only life-raft and chance to get to paradise. This is because if society wasn't so sinful and so immoral then Christians would have no target audience desperate for a saviour because they'd realize God can just forgive them. Sinful societies promote Christianity. Moral societies are athema to Christian proselytization. If people weren't "hopeless sinners" they wouldn't think they need to be "saved" with a fatal sacrifice paid with the blood of God and/or his son. Only if everyone is really wicked can Christianity make a case for the bloody atonement via Christ. If people "aren't that bad" we don't need God to bleed and die for us, so this is why Christians inherently promote sin even if it's unintentional because their theology requires evil societies or nobody would ever accept Christianity as plausible in any way. Politicians and Clergy know this and that's why clergy rarely/barely complain when politicians create sinful societies because the clergy knows sinful societies help them preach and get people involved with Christianity. The clergy also likes war because then they can pray for peace. During war lots of people go to church to pray, and while in church they tend to make monetary donations as well. If the world is not a sinful evil immoral place filled with evildoers then Christians have no salespitch they can make. This is why governments historically have been very friendly with clergy. It's a symbiotic relationship. Hence this is why the Roman Empire actually became more degenerate AFTER Christianity spread throughout it, because even the pagans had a moral code of conduct but Pauline Christianity gave states a blank check to cultivate sin as unofficial policy. Do the research, <u>the Roman Empire and morality declined as the citizenry converted from Paganism to Christianity</u>. **Thus Christians were and are generally more immoral than polytheistic Pagan Idolaters**. Christianity was and is a religion where governments of Christian peoples never actually have to morally reform and improve their citizens because Christian clerics need and subconsciously desire the opposite. Except for the rare minority who actually believe and try practicing the minute level of morality they preach. Governments + Christianity = the economics of sin + a theological necessity for an economy/nation based upon sinfulness. But worst of all Christians claim adherence to genuine prophets while preaching creeds contradicting the core message of God's prophetic faith. In my opinion, as a former Christian, someone claiming a prophet is God or a son of God and that such a being died as a sin transferring sacrifice is worse than someone disbelieving in a prophet and practicing polytheism; though both false faiths lead the practitioner to eternal hellfire.

If you read the gospel of Barnabas, which is not included in the New Testament, it has a different version of Judas' betrayal that includes 30 gold pieces instead of silver, saying that Jesus was saved by God and taken to paradise when Judas came to betray him. Judas went into a house where Jesus and his apostles were, including Barnabas, late at night in order to confirm that Jesus was there. The roman soldiers didn't know what Jesus looked like which is why they needed someone to confirm his whereabouts, since they wouldn't be able to recognize Jesus even if they saw him. The gospel of Barnabas says that Jesus was taken by angels to paradise out of the house and Judas was physically transformed to look like Jesus. The roman soldiers took Judas not believing him when he said what happened, while the apostles who witnessed the ascension of Jesus and Judas' transformation didn't stand up on Judas' behalf. Judas having been made to look like Jesus started to realize how he would get the punishment he intended to bring upon Jesus and pleaded his case maintaining he wasn't who they thought. They took Judas to Herod Antipas and then Pontius Pilate hoping to get a ruling, because it was illegal to execute an insane person. If it was Jesus thinking he was Judas they couldn't kill him and if it was Judas then they'd be punishing someone they didn't intend to, either way it'd be illegal. Eventually the gospel says they crucified Judas thinking it was Jesus with God giving the traitor the suffering he intended for the prophet as a way of justice. While this gospel is not 100% verified, it is as authentic as the 4 canonical gospels, so you can take it with a grain of salt. The gospel of Barnabas was for a time on the fringe of the canon. Clement of Alexandria regarded it sufficiently important to write a commentary on it in his *Hypotyposes*, which is now inaccessible and lost to us. Origen called it '*catholic*', a term that he also applied to 1 Peter and 1 John. In the fourth-century Codex Sinaiticus of the Greek Bible the gospel of Barnabas stands after the New Testament. Irenaeus would frequently quote this gospel as an authoritative text. The main reason it lost popularity was because after the council of Nicaea in 325 CE Pope Damasus told people it was forbidden to read it. Why? Well he was the Pope, that's why, if the Pope said don't read X then X was not read and it would get destroyed. Yet he didn't have any scholarly reasons for rejecting it, he just didn't agree with it and assumed he was right so that must mean it was wrong. Rather than refute it he just said "don't read it" because it didn't agree with his beliefs about Jesus or the alleged crucifixion. The 4 canonical gospels themselves don't agree on the alleged crucifixion. Some say Jesus was crucified on Thursday, others say on Friday, that's a big discrepancy. Imagine your best friend and leader who is a prophet gets killed by the government, you're going to remember what day it is and so will all the other followers of the prophet. It couldn't have happened multiple days at different times. The gospels not only disagree on the time, but they disagree on the place of the alleged resurrection as well. The 4 canonical gospels also disagree on the alleged last words. Some say Jesus said, "*My God, My God, why have you forsaken me?*" This is actually a biblical statement of disbelief, Jewish theology taught that when God abandoned people due to disbelief compounded by major sins they would say this phrase. The bible contains this catchphrase and its used when a prophet or righteous person became a disbeliever in God. That's another thing many don't know, in that Jewish theology and the Old Testament teaches that certain prophets like David disbelieved. (They claim that as a prophet he tried to murder a believer he was sent to teach because as a prophet he allegedly committed adultery with that guy's wife.) Of course Jews then say David was guided back into belief after repenting and vowing to change, but for this phrase to be one's "last words" meant guaranteed eternal damnation in the hellfire. Jesus could not possibly say these words, especially if he was the Lord as part of a trinity. On the other hand Judas would be prone to make such a statement if he were made to look like Jesus and crucified as the gospel of Barnabas says. There are other alternate crucifixion versions in other gospels that didn't make it into the bible as well. One has Simon the Cypriote, who is said to have helped carry the cross, switching places with Jesus and having Simon crucified instead. We are told that Jesus had to carry the cross for the sins of mankind, yet the bible says that a guy called Simon carried the cross for most of the way. Carrying the cross one is to be killed on itself is entirely foreign to the execution style of crucifixion and no one who was crucified had ever done it. It would be like a person sentenced to be hanged having to tie their own noose, or having to build the very electric chair that is going to electrocute you. Also if someone I loved were executed I would not glorify the instrument of their destruction by wearing an electric chair around my neck or some other gruesome miniature of the device which caused their death, but Christians glorify crosses and wear them. Christians also say the crucifixion of Jesus was a good thing that resulted in their salvation. If they truly believe that then why do they vilify Judas who they believe sent Jesus to that fate? If Judas is the one who got Jesus crucified thereby ensuring their salvation, they should consider Judas a saint. Yet despite all the various statues Christians have erected in their churches, none of them have a monument of Judas praising him for his role in the alleged crucifixion.

One key to remember is that even if the biblical gospels agreed, which they don't, they were not written by eyewitnesses and they were written in Greek, a language other than that of Jesus and his companions, long after the events in question. For more information on the fallibility and lack of holiness of the bibles I refer you to my books "Which edition of the bible is from God?" or "A Muslim Analysis of the bible".

What do the Jews have to say about Jesus? Most Christians never bother to ask, why bother asking the accused about the crime they've been are accused of? They just use the Guantanamo approach, in that they wouldn't have been accused if they weren't guilty, even though the U.S. government itself has released hundreds of detainees after years of torture without charges saying they were actually innocent all along. Well today Jews let the Christians think the Romans did it because they don't want to get slaughtered by Christians as they did in the past. However any Jewish Scholar or Rabbi familiar with the Talmud and Jewish history knows that up until very recently the Jewish position was that the Romans had nothing to do with Jesus departing at all. The Jews proudly claimed 100% responsibility, but guess what? They say that Jesus was legally convicted in a Jewish Rabbinical court for promoting contempt for Rabbinical authority and was therefore stoned to death. The Jews say there were no crosses, no stakes and no Romans. The Jews said that they and they alone stoned Jesus to death. Ultimately God knows best what really happened to Jesus.

The Muslim belief comes from the Quran 4:150-159:

إِنَّ ٱلَّذِينَ يَكْفُرُونَ بِٱللَّهِ وَرُسُلِهِ وَيُرِيدُونَ أَن يُفَرِّقُوا بَيْنَ ٱللَّهِ وَرُسُلِهِ وَيَقُولُونَ نُؤْمِنُ بِبَعْضٍ وَنَكْفُرُ بِبَعْضٍ وَيُرِيدُونَ أَن يَتَّخِذُوا بَيْنَ ذَٰلِكَ سَبِيلًا (١٥٠) أُو۟لَـٰٓئِكَ هُمُ ٱلْكَـٰفِرُونَ حَقًّا وَأَعْتَدْنَا لِلْكَـٰفِرِينَ عَذَابًا مُّهِينًا (١٥١) وَٱلَّذِينَ ءَامَنُوا بِٱللَّهِ وَرُسُلِهِ وَلَمْ يُفَرِّقُوا بَيْنَ أَحَدٍ مِّنْهُمْ أُو۟لَـٰٓئِكَ سَوْفَ يُؤْتِيهِمْ أُجُورَهُمْ وَكَانَ ٱللَّهُ غَفُورًا رَّحِيمًا (١٥٢) يَسْـَٔلُكَ أَهْلُ ٱلْكِتَـٰبِ أَن تُنَزِّلَ عَلَيْهِمْ كِتَـٰبًا مِّنَ ٱلسَّمَآءِ فَقَدْ سَأَلُوا مُوسَىٰٓ أَكْبَرَ مِن ذَٰلِكَ فَقَالُوٓا أَرِنَا ٱللَّهَ جَهْرَةً فَأَخَذَتْهُمُ ٱلصَّـٰعِقَةُ بِظُلْمِهِمْ ثُمَّ ٱتَّخَذُوا ٱلْعِجْلَ مِنۢ بَعْدِ مَا جَآءَتْهُمُ ٱلْبَيِّنَـٰتُ فَعَفَوْنَا عَن ذَٰلِكَ وَءَاتَيْنَا مُوسَىٰ سُلْطَـٰنًا مُّبِينًا (١٥٣) وَرَفَعْنَا فَوْقَهُمُ ٱلطُّورَ بِمِيثَـٰقِهِمْ وَقُلْنَا لَهُمُ ٱدْخُلُوا ٱلْبَابَ سُجَّدًا وَقُلْنَا لَهُمْ لَا تَعْدُوا فِى ٱلسَّبْتِ وَأَخَذْنَا مِنْهُم مِّيثَـٰقًا غَلِيظًا (١٥٤) فَبِمَا نَقْضِهِم مِّيثَـٰقَهُمْ وَكُفْرِهِم بِـَٔايَـٰتِ ٱللَّهِ وَقَتْلِهِمُ ٱلْأَنۢبِيَآءَ بِغَيْرِ حَقٍّ وَقَوْلِهِمْ قُلُوبُنَا غُلْفٌۢ بَلْ طَبَعَ ٱللَّهُ عَلَيْهَا بِكُفْرِهِمْ فَلَا يُؤْمِنُونَ إِلَّا قَلِيلًا (١٥٥) وَبِكُفْرِهِمْ وَقَوْلِهِمْ عَلَىٰ مَرْيَمَ بُهْتَـٰنًا عَظِيمًا (١٥٦) وَقَوْلِهِمْ إِنَّا قَتَلْنَا ٱلْمَسِيحَ عِيسَى ٱبْنَ مَرْيَمَ رَسُولَ ٱللَّهِ وَمَا قَتَلُوهُ وَمَا صَلَبُوهُ وَلَـٰكِن شُبِّهَ لَهُمْ وَإِنَّ ٱلَّذِينَ ٱخْتَلَفُوا فِيهِ لَفِى شَكٍّۢ مِّنْهُ مَا لَهُم بِهِۦ مِنْ عِلْمٍ إِلَّا ٱتِّبَاعَ ٱلظَّنِّ وَمَا قَتَلُوهُ يَقِينًۢا (١٥٧) بَل رَّفَعَهُ ٱللَّهُ إِلَيْهِ وَكَانَ ٱللَّهُ عَزِيزًا حَكِيمًا (١٥٨) وَإِن مِّنْ أَهْلِ ٱلْكِتَـٰبِ إِلَّا لَيُؤْمِنَنَّ بِهِۦ قَبْلَ مَوْتِهِۦ وَيَوْمَ ٱلْقِيَـٰمَةِ يَكُونُ عَلَيْهِمْ شَهِيدًا (١٥٩)

"Those who deny Allah and His Messengers, and (those who) wish to separate Allah and His Messengers, saying: "We believe in some but reject others": and (those who) wish to take a course midway. They are in truth (equally) Unbelievers; and We have prepared for unbelievers a humiliating punishment. To those who believe in

*Allah and His messenger and make no distinction between any of the messengers, We shall soon give their (due) rewards: for Allah is Oft-Forgiving, Most Merciful. The people of the Book ask thee to cause a book to descend to them from heaven: indeed they asked Moses for an even greater (miracle), for they said: "Show us Allah in public" but they were dazed for their presumption, by thunder and lightning. Yet they worshipped the calf even after clear signs had come to them; even so We forgave them; and gave Moses manifest proofs of authority. And for their Covenant We raised over them (the towering height) of Mount (Sinai); and (on another occasion) We said: "Enter the gate with humility"; and (once again) We commanded them: "Transgress not in the matter of the Sabbath." And We took from them a solemn Covenant. (They have incurred divine displeasure): in that they broke their Covenant: that they rejected the Signs of Allah; that they slew the Messengers in defiance of right; that they said "Our hearts are the wrappings (which preserve Allah's Word; we need no more)"; nay Allah hath set the seal on their hearts for their blasphemy, and little is it they believe. That **they rejected Faith: that they uttered against Mary a grave false charge. That they said (in boast), "We killed Christ Jesus the son of Mary, the Messenger of Allah"; but they killed him not, nor crucified him, but so it was made to appear to them and those who differ therein are full of doubts, with no (certain) knowledge, but only conjecture to follow, for of a surety they killed him not. Nay, Allah raised him up unto Himself; and Allah is Exalted in Power, Wise.** And there is none of the People of the Book but must believe in him before his death; and on the Day of Judgment He (Jesus) will be a witness against them."*

The scholar Ibn Kathir wrote about the Muslim belief in his Tafsir (commentary on the Quran):

"Ibn Abi Hatim recorded that Ibn `Abbas said: "Just before Allah raised `Jesus to the heavens, `Jesus went to his companions, who were twelve inside the house. When he arrived, his hair was dripping water and he said, `There are those among you who will disbelieve in me twelve times after he had believed in me.' He then asked, 'Who volunteers that his image appear as mine, and be killed in my place. He will be with me (in Paradise)' One of the youngest ones among them volunteered and `Jesus asked him to sit down. `Jesus again asked for a volunteer, and the young man kept volunteering and `Jesus asking him to sit down. Then the young man volunteered again and `Jesus said, `You will be that man,' and the resemblance of `Jesus was cast over that man while `Jesus ascended to heaven from a hole in the house. When the Jews came looking for `Jesus, they found that young man and crucified him. Some of `Jesus' followers disbelieved in him twelve times after they had believed in him. They then divided into three groups. One group, Al-Ya`qubiyyah (Jacobites), said, `Allah remained with us as long as He willed and then ascended to heaven.' Another group, An-Nasturiyyah (Nestorians), said, `The son of Allah was with us as long as he willed and Allah took him to heaven.' Another group, Muslims, said, `The servant and Messenger of Allah remained with us as long as Allah willed, and Allah then took him to

Him.' The two disbelieving groups cooperated against the Muslim group and they killed them. Ever since that happened, Islam was then veiled until Allah sent Muhammad." This statement has an authentic chain of narration leading to Ibn `Abbas, and An-Nasa'i narrated it through Abu Kurayb who reported it from Abu Mu`awiyah."

The scholar al-Baydawi commented in his tafsir of these verses similarily saying:

There is a story that a group of Jews insulted Jesus and his mother, whereupon he appealed to God against them. When God transformed those [who had insulted them] into monkeys and swine, the Jews took counsel to kill Jesus. Then God told Jesus that He would raise him up to heaven, and so <u>Jesus said to his disciples: "Who among you will agree to take a form similar to mine and die [in my place] and be crucified and then go [straight] to paradise?"</u> A man among them offered himself, so God changed him into a form resembling Jesus' and he was killed and crucified.

<u>Others say that a man pretended [to be a believer] in Jesus' presence but then went off and denounced him, whereupon God changed the man into a form similar to that of Jesus, and that he was seized and crucified</u>.

It was also narrated that Ibn 'Abbas said:

"There were kings after 'Isa(Jesus) bin Mariam who altered the Tawrah and the Injil, but there were among them believers who read the Tawrah. It was said to their kings: 'We have never heard of any slander worse than that of those (believers) who slander us and recite: "And whosoever does not judge by what Allah has revealed, such are the disbelievers." In these Verses, they are criticizing us for our deeds when they recite them.' So he called them together and gave them the choice between being put to death, or giving up reading the Tawrah and Injil, except for what had been altered. They said: 'Why do you want us to change? Leave us alone.' Some of them said: 'Build us a tower and let us go up there, and give us something to lift up our food and drink so we do not have to mix with you.' Others said: 'Let us go and wander throughout the land, and we will drink as the wild animals drink, and if you capture us in your land, you may kill us.' Others said: 'Build houses for us in the wilderness, and we will dig wells and grow vegetables, and we will not mix with you or pass by you, for there is no one of the tribes among whom we do not have close relatives.' So they did that, and Allah revealed the words: 'But the monasticism which they invented for themselves, We did not prescribe for them, but (they sought it) only to please Allah therewith, but that they did not observe it with the right observance.' Then others said: 'We will worship as so-and-so worshipped, and we will wander as so-and-so wandered, and we will adopt houses (in the wilderness) as so-and-so did.' But they were still following their Shirk with no knowledge of the faith of those whom they claimed to be following. When Allah sent the Prophet(Muhammad), and they were only a few of them left, a man came down from his cell, and a wanderer came from his travels, and a monk came from his monastery, and they believed in him. And Allah said: 'O you who believe! Fear Allah, and believe in His Messenger, He will give you a double portion *of His mercy - meaning, two rewards, because of their having believed in 'Isa (Jesus) and in the Tawrah and Injil, and for having believing in Muhammad; and He will give you a light by which you shall walk (straight), - meaning, the Qur'an, and their following the Prophet; and He said: 'So that the people of the Scripture (Jews and Christians) may know that they have no power whatsoever over the Grace of Allah.'"*

Source: Sunan an-Nasa'i 5400 Graded Daif by Darussalam

    People will say all the contradicting biblical verses and different viewpoints of the writers don't matter or change the message. They do, but for the sake of argument we'll say they don't. Now these same people will say the bible is the "*word of God*", the less fanatical will say "*the inspired word of God*". That changes everything, because only one version of an event can be true. God knows exactly what happened and has no confusion about it. If God inspired people to write different versions of what happened, some of which are contradicting each other, then that would mean God is telling one thing to one person and another thing to someone else. God does not lie. With different viewpoints/versions it causes confusion, since God wants us to worship him there wouldn't be any divine jokes being played or games where you have to find out which gospel is right and which isn't. God makes it plain for us to know what is right and what is wrong, it's Satan, Jinn and people who make things confusing. Since there are indeed different versions describing the same events in the bible, it cannot all be the word of God or inspired by God. To claim so is to say God was a liar and to call God a liar makes one a disbeliever. I don't mean to bash the bible, that's not my intention. There are many good advices inside of it and it still has some essence of the religion of the prophets, unfortunately there are also some bad advices, as well as false information. The bible also contains things of which the authenticity cannot be verified or trusted. I'm only bringing this information to your attention because the bible is important and remains a powerful influence around the world today, which sends people in many different directions. Therefore it's crucial to understand the bible correctly for what it is. We are all brothers and sisters in humanity and if you were in my position with access to this information I would want you to share it with me, so please do not have hard feelings towards me for sharing. I know personally this information is very hard to digest and shakes one to the core arousing much emotion. Satan uses our passions against us over and over again. Please don't dismiss this based on your emotional reaction, an intellectual exertion must be made in order to process this in a healthy manner. Without a doubt Jesus is a very important prophet. There is another important verse from Matthew concerning what will happen when specific individuals meet Jesus on the Day of Judgement. The bible allegedly records the exact words which those specific individuals will utter with their lips on that day. In context biblical Jesus is telling people what is predestined to occur for specific individuals who weren't even born at that time but because of their freewill choices they will make in life and God's knowledge of everything in totality the biblical Jesus is said to have said in Matthew 7:22-23, "*²² Many will say to me on that day, 'Lord, Lord, did we not prophesy in your name and in your name drive out demons and in your name perform many miracles?' ²³ Then* **I will tell them plainly, 'I never knew you. Away from me, you evildoers!'**" These verses in Matthew have Jesus saying how he will reject certain people and refuse to be with them in the afterlife. These people he is talking about are not Jews, Muslims, Hindus, Buddhists or Atheists. These people will come to Jesus and say: "Lord, Lord, did we not prophesy in your name and in your name drive out demons and in your name perform many miracles?" Now if everyone from all time was transported to the Day of Judgement right this minute what kind of people would call Jesus "Lord" and say to him that they did things in his name? Christians. It is Christians whom the bible says Jesus will tell, "I never knew you. Away from me, you evildoers!" Why would Jesus say this? Because they called Jesus their Lord/savior and prayed to Jesus or in the name of Jesus instead of God mistakenly thinking he had power to intercede with God, was a son of God, and/or that he was killed for their sins. Whereas because that is a slander and type of backbiting against Jesus then Christians rather than having Jesus pay the price for their debt(sins) they are actually indebted to Jesus for having slandered and backbit him and must pay the price with either good deeds or accepting the victim's sins on their record. Meaning Jesus can legally have his sins get transferred to them in a form of ironic justice/revenge, such Christians will be completely surprised when faced with the reality of burning in hell for disbelief in Jesus and having his sins added to their burden if he so chooses which he might choose to do. So Christians who claim Jesus died for their sins may in fact burn in hell because of having the sins of Jesus transferred to them for their crime of blasphemy, backbiting and slander. Christians could pay the price in hell for the sins of Jesus rather than the other way around as they preach. These Christians, who gave so much in charity, built hospitals and orphanages, when they meet Jesus in the afterlife will hear a similar greeting as in Matthew 4:10 ,"*¹⁰ Jesus said to him, "Away from me, Satan! For* it is written: '**Worship the Lord your God, and serve him only**.'" Muhammad taught the same, there is none to be worshiped but God the Creator, alone without any partners. There are no middlemen between the creation and the Creator. Sins are not transferable. Everyone earns their own ticket to paradise paying the price themselves. All prayers are for the Creator alone. Prayer is a form of worship, any prayer done to someone or something else or in the name of someone or something else is considered to be worshipping something or someone else. In Islam it is forbidden to pray to something that prays, and everything prays except for the Creator of all things. The fact is that Jesus is a Muslim prophet, born via a miraculous virgin birth, who never died yet and will return. The Quran even mentions Mary mother of Jesus more times than the bible does and has a whole chapter named after her. As a former Catholic Seminarian I now believe with certain confident conviction that Muhammad pbuh was sent by God to fix the corruptions of the Christians and others regarding Jesus and the religion of the prophets. Islam is the true faith though each individual Muslim varies in their adherence to orthodoxy or salafiyyah. To learn more you have to do more research. For an accurate understanding of Jesus' teachings I refer you to my book "The Collection of Quotes Credited to Prophet Jesus". I will end this book with information Muhammad pbuh conveyed about Jesus pbuh in authentic hadiths before concluding with a challenge from the Quran which offers a solution to the dispute between Muslims and Christians regarding the truth about Jesus pbuh. In summary, you now know there is Contradicting Biblical Conjecture and the origin of the belief in a semi-divine being's savioral crucifixion is ancient pagan mythology.

Sahih Bukhari Volume 3, Book 34, Number 425: Narrated Abu Huraira: Allah's Messenger said:

"By Him in Whose Hands my soul is, son of Mary (Jesus) will shortly descend amongst you people (Muslims) as a just ruler and will break the Cross and kill the pig and abolish the Jizya (a tax taken from the non-Muslims, who are in the protection, of the Muslim government). Then there will be abundance of money and no-body will accept charitable gifts.

Sahih Bukhari Volume 3, Book 43, Number 656: Narrated Abu Huraira: Allah's Messenger said:

"The Hour will not be established until the son of Mary (i.e. Jesus) descends amongst you as a just ruler, he will break the cross, kill the pigs, and abolish the Jizya tax. Money will be in abundance so that nobody will accept it (as charitable gifts).

Sahih Bukhari Volume 4, Book 54, Number 506: Narrated Abu Huraira: The Prophet said:

"When any human being is born. Satan touches him at both sides of the body with his two fingers, except Jesus, the son of Mary, whom Satan tried to touch but failed, for he touched the placenta-cover instead."

Sahih Bukhari Volume 4, Book 55, Number 640: Narrated Malik bin Sasaa: That the Prophet talked to them about the night of his Ascension to the Heavens. He said:

"(Then Gabriel took me) and ascended up till he reached the second heaven where he asked for the gate to be opened, but it was asked, 'Who is it?' Gabriel replied, 'I am Gabriel.' It was asked, 'Who is accompanying you?' He replied, 'Muhammad.' It was asked, 'Has he been called?' He said, 'Yes.' When we reached over the second

heaven, I saw Yahya (i.e. John) and Jesus who were cousins. Gabriel said, 'These are John (Yahya) and Jesus, so greet them.' I greeted them and they returned the greeting saying, 'Welcome, O Pious Brother and Pious Prophet!;' "

Sahih Bukhari Volume 4, Book 55, Number 647: Narrated Abu Huraira: The Prophet said:

"I met Moses on the night of my Ascension to heaven." The Prophet then described him saying, as I think, "He was a tall person with lank hair as if he belonged to the people of the tribe of Shanu's.' The Prophet further said, "I met Jesus." The Prophet described him saying, "He was one of moderate height and was red-faced as if he had just come out of a bathroom. I saw Abraham whom I resembled more than any of his children did." The Prophet further said, "(That night) I was given two cups; one full of milk and the other full of wine. I was asked to take either of them which I liked, and I took the milk and drank it. On that it was said to me, 'You have taken the right path (religion). If you had taken the wine, your (Muslim) nation would have gone astray."

Sahih Bukhari Volume 4, Book 55, Number 648: Narrated Ibn Umar: The Prophet said:

"I saw Moses, Jesus and Abraham (on the night of my Ascension to the heavens). Jesus was of red complexion, curly hair and a broad chest. Moses was of brown complexion, straight hair and tall stature as if he was from the people of Az-Zutt."

Sahih Buhkari Volume 4, Book 55, Number 651: Narrated Abu Huraira: I heard Allah's Messenger saying:

"I am the nearest of all the people to the son of Mary, and all the prophets are paternal brothers, and there has been no prophet between me and him (i.e. Jesus)."

Sahih Bukhari Volume 4, Book 55, Number 652: Narrated Abu Huraira: Allah's Messenger said:

"Both in this world and in the Hereafter, I am the nearest of all the people to Jesus, the son of Mary. The prophets are paternal brothers; their mothers are different, but their religion is one."

Sahih Bukhari Volume 4, Book 55, Number 655: Narrated Abu Musa Al-Ash'ari: Allah's Messenger said:

"If a person teaches his slave girl good manners properly, educates her properly, and then manumits and marries her, he will get a double reward. And if a man believes in Jesus and then believes in me, he will get a double reward. And if a slave fears his Lord (i.e. Allah) and obeys his masters, he too will get a double reward."

Sahih Bukhari Volume 4, Book 55, Number 657: Narrated Abu Huraira: Allah's Messenger said:

"By Him in Whose Hands my soul is, surely (Jesus,) the son of Mary will soon descend amongst you and will judge mankind justly (as a Just Ruler); he will break the Cross and kill the pigs and there will be no Jizya (i.e. taxation taken from non Muslims). Money will be in abundance so that nobody will accept it, and a single prostration to Allah (in prayer) will be better than the whole world and whatever is in it." Abu Huraira added "If you wish, you can recite (this verse of the Holy Book): -- 'And there is none Of the people of the Scriptures (Jews and Christians) But must believe in him (i.e Jesus as an Apostle of Allah and a human being) Before his death. And on the Day of Judgment He will be a witness Against them." (4.159)

Sahih Bukhari Volume 4, Book 55, Number 658: Narrated Abu Huraira: Allah's Messenger said:

"How will you be when the son of Mary (i.e. Jesus) descends amongst you and he will judge people by the Law of the Quran and not by the law of Gospel."

Sahih Bukhari Volume 6, Book 60, Number 3: Narrated Anas: The Prophet said:

"On the Day of Resurrection the Believers will assemble and say, 'Let us ask somebody to intercede for us with our Lord.' So they will go to Adam and say, 'You are the father of all the people, and Allah created you with His Own Hands, and ordered the angels to prostrate to you, and taught you the names of all things; so please intercede for us with your Lord, so that He may relieve us from this place of ours.' Adam will say, 'I am not fit for this (i.e. intercession for you).' Then Adam will remember his sin and feel ashamed thereof. He will say, 'Go to Noah, for he was the first Apostle, Allah sent to the inhabitants of the earth.' They will go to him and Noah will say, 'I am not fit for this undertaking.' He will remember his appeal to his Lord to do what he had no knowledge of, then he will feel ashamed thereof and will say, 'Go to the Khalil--r-Rahman (i.e. Abraham).' They will go to him and he will say, 'I am not fit for this undertaking. Go to Moses, the slave to whom Allah spoke (directly) and gave him the Torah .' So they will go to him and he will say, 'I am not fit for this undertaking.' and he will mention (his) killing a person who was not a killer, and so he will feel ashamed thereof before his Lord, and he will say, 'Go to Jesus, Allah's Slave, His Apostle and Allah's Word and a Spirit coming from Him. Jesus will say, 'I am not fit for this undertaking, go to Muhammad the Slave of Allah whose past and future sins were forgiven by Allah.' So they will come to me and I will proceed till I will ask my Lord's Permission and I will be given permission. When I see my Lord, I will fall down in Prostration and He will let me remain in that state as long as He wishes and then I will be addressed.' (Muhammad!) Raise your head. Ask, and your request will be granted; say, and your saying will be listened to; intercede, and your intercession will be accepted.' I will raise my head and praise Allah with a saying (i.e. invocation) He will teach me, and then I will intercede. He will fix a limit for me (to intercede for) whom I will admit into Paradise. Then I will come back again to Allah, and when I see my Lord, the same thing will happen to me. And then I will intercede and Allah will fix a limit for me to intercede whom I will let into Paradise, then I will come back for the third time; and then I will come back for the fourth time, and will say, 'None remains in Hell but those whom the Quran has imprisoned (in Hell) and who have been destined to an eternal stay in Hell.' " (The compiler) Abu 'Abdullah said: 'But those whom the Qur'an has imprisoned in Hell,' refers to the Statement of Allah: "They will dwell therein forever." (16.29)

Sunan Abi Dawud 4324   Narrated Abu Hurayrah:
The Prophet (ﷺ) said: *There is no prophet between me and him, that is, Jesus. He will descent (to the earth). When you see him, recognise him: a man of medium height, reddish fair, wearing two light yellow garments, looking as if drops were falling down from his head though it will not be wet. He will fight the people for the cause of Islam. He will break the cross, kill swine, and abolish jizyah. Allah will perish all religions except Islam. He will destroy the Antichrist and will live on the earth for forty years and then he will die. The Muslims will pray over him.*

Grade: Sahih

Riyad as-Salihin 412   'Ubadah bin As-Samit reported:
Messenger of Allah (ﷺ) said, "*He who bears witness that there is no true god except Allah, alone having no partner with Him, that Muhammad is His slave and His Messenger, that 'Isa (Jesus) is His slave and Messenger and he (Jesus) is His Word which He communicated to Maryam (Mary) and His spirit which He sent to her, that Paradise is true and Hell is true; Allah will make him enter Paradise accepting whatever deeds he accomplished*".

Grade: Sahih

Quran 10:36

وَمَا يَتَّبِعُ أَكْثَرُهُمْ إِلَّا ظَنًّا ۚ إِنَّ ٱلظَّنَّ لَا يُغْنِى مِنَ ٱلْحَقِّ شَيْـًٔا ۚ إِنَّ ٱللَّهَ عَلِيمٌۢ بِمَا يَفْعَلُونَ

And most of them follow nothing but conjecture. Certainly, conjecture can be of no avail against the truth. Surely, Allâh is All-Aware of what they do. (36)

Quran 3:54-64

وَمَكَرُواْ وَمَكَرَ ٱللَّهُ ۖ وَٱللَّهُ خَيْرُ ٱلْمَٰكِرِينَ (٥٤) إِذْ قَالَ ٱللَّهُ يَٰعِيسَىٰٓ إِنِّى مُتَوَفِّيكَ وَرَافِعُكَ إِلَىَّ وَمُطَهِّرُكَ مِنَ ٱلَّذِينَ كَفَرُواْ وَجَاعِلُ ٱلَّذِينَ ٱتَّبَعُوكَ فَوْقَ ٱلَّذِينَ كَفَرُوٓاْ إِلَىٰ يَوْمِ ٱلْقِيَٰمَةِ ۖ ثُمَّ إِلَىَّ

مَرْجِعُكُمْ فَأَحْكُمُ بَيْنَكُمْ فِيمَا كُنتُمْ فِيهِ تَخْتَلِفُونَ (٥٥) فَأَمَّا ٱلَّذِينَ كَفَرُواْ فَأُعَذِّبُهُمْ عَذَابًا شَدِيدًا فِى ٱلدُّنْيَا وَٱلْأَخِرَةِ وَمَا لَهُم مِّن نَّـٰصِرِينَ (٥٦) وَأَمَّا ٱلَّذِينَ ءَامَنُواْ وَعَمِلُواْ ٱلصَّـٰلِحَـٰتِ فَيُوَفِّيهِمْ أُجُورَهُمْ وَٱللَّهُ لَا يُحِبُّ ٱلظَّـٰلِمِينَ (٥٧) ذَٰلِكَ نَتْلُوهُ عَلَيْكَ مِنَ ٱلْـَٔايَـٰتِ وَٱلذِّكْرِ ٱلْحَكِيمِ (٥٨) إِنَّ مَثَلَ عِيسَىٰ عِندَ ٱللَّهِ كَمَثَلِ ءَادَمَ خَلَقَهُۥ مِن تُرَابٍۢ ثُمَّ قَالَ لَهُۥ كُن فَيَكُونُ (٥٩) ٱلْحَقُّ مِن رَّبِّكَ فَلَا تَكُن مِّنَ ٱلْمُمْتَرِينَ (٦٠) فَمَنْ حَآجَّكَ فِيهِ مِنۢ بَعْدِ مَا جَآءَكَ مِنَ ٱلْعِلْمِ فَقُلْ تَعَالَوْاْ نَدْعُ أَبْنَآءَنَا وَأَبْنَآءَكُمْ وَنِسَآءَنَا وَنِسَآءَكُمْ وَأَنفُسَنَا وَأَنفُسَكُمْ ثُمَّ نَبْتَهِلْ فَنَجْعَل لَّعْنَتَ ٱللَّهِ عَلَى ٱلْكَـٰذِبِينَ (٦١) إِنَّ هَـٰذَا لَهُوَ ٱلْقَصَصُ ٱلْحَقُّ وَمَا مِنْ إِلَـٰهٍ إِلَّا ٱللَّهُ وَإِنَّ ٱللَّهَ لَهُوَ ٱلْعَزِيزُ ٱلْحَكِيمُ (٦٢) فَإِن تَوَلَّوْاْ فَإِنَّ ٱللَّهَ عَلِيمٌۢ بِٱلْمُفْسِدِينَ (٦٣) قُلْ يَـٰٓأَهْلَ ٱلْكِتَـٰبِ تَعَالَوْاْ إِلَىٰ كَلِمَةٍۢ سَوَآءٍۭ بَيْنَنَا وَبَيْنَكُمْ أَلَّا نَعْبُدَ إِلَّا ٱللَّهَ وَلَا نُشْرِكَ بِهِۦ شَيْـًٔا وَلَا يَتَّخِذَ بَعْضُنَا بَعْضًا أَرْبَابًۭا مِّن دُونِ ٱللَّهِ فَإِن تَوَلَّوْاْ فَقُولُواْ ٱشْهَدُواْ بِأَنَّا مُسْلِمُونَ (٦٤)

And they (disbelievers) plotted [to kill 'Īsā (Jesus)], and Allâh plotted too. And Allâh is the Best of those who plot. (54) And (remember) when Allâh said: "O 'Īsā (Jesus)! I will take you and raise you to Myself and clear you [of the forged statement that 'Īsā (Jesus) is Allâh's son] of those who disbelieve, and I will make those who follow you (Monotheists, who worship none but Allâh) superior to those who disbelieve [in the Oneness of Allâh, or disbelieve in some of His Messengers, e.g. Muhammad, 'Īsā (Jesus), Mûsâ (Moses), etc., or in His Holy Books, e.g. the Taurât (Torah), the Injeel, the Qur'ân] till the Day of Resurrection. Then you will return to Me and I will judge between you in the matters in which you used to dispute." (55) "As to those who disbelieve, I will punish them with a severe torment in this world and in the Hereafter, and they will have no helpers." (56) And as for those who believe (in the Oneness of Allâh) and do righteous good deeds, Allâh will pay them their reward in full. And Allâh does not like the Zâlimûn (polytheists and wrong-doers). (57) This is what We recite to you (O Muhammad) of the Verses and the Wise Reminder (i.e. the Qur'ân) (58) Verily, **the likeness of 'Īsā (Jesus) before Allâh is the likeness of Adam. He created him from dust, then (He) said to him: "Be!" - and he was**. (59) (This is) the truth from your Lord, so be not of those who doubt. (60) Then **whoever disputes with you concerning him ['Īsā (Jesus)] after (all this) knowledge that has come to you**, [i.e. 'Īsā (Jesus)] being a slave of Allâh, and having no share in Divinity) **say**: (O Muhammad) "**Come, let us call our sons and your sons, our women and your women, ourselves and yourselves - then we pray and invoke (sincerely) the Curse of Allâh upon those who lie.**" (61) Verily! This is the true narrative [about the story of 'Īsā (Jesus)], and, Lâ ilâha ill-Allâh (none has the right to be worshipped but Allâh, the One and the Only True God, Who has neither a wife nor a son). And indeed, Allâh is the All-Mighty, the All-Wise.

(62)And _**if they turn away**_ (and do not accept these true proofs and evidences), then surely, Allâh is All-Aware of those who do mischief. (63)Say (O Muhammad): "O people of the Scripture (Jews and Christians): Come to a word that is just between us and you, that we worship none but Allâh (Alone), and that we associate no partners with Him, and that none of us shall take others as lords besides Allâh. Then, _if they turn away, say_: "_**Bear witness that we are Muslims**_." (64)

www.ingramcontent.com/pod-product-compliance
Lightning Source LLC
Chambersburg PA
CBHW060406010526
44107CB00005B/603